FLORIDA PERMACULTURE GARDENING

TRANSFORM YOUR BARREN BACKYARD INTO A HIGH YIELDING ORGANIC ECOSYSTEM

VIOLET MALONE

Contents

ACKNOWLEDGMENT

To Crow.
Thank you for being such an amazing coach, mentor and most importantly, a friend.
You will be missed.

In the "10 budget friendly Gardening HACKS", you'll discover...

The ultimate 10 affordable and surprising gardening hacks

Plus, 3 bonuses!

1. Top 5 survival plants everyone should have in their garden

2. How to test your soil pH with a kit: step by step guide

3. List of tools and equipment you and your garden can't live without

Download it here: *Violetmalone.com*

Introduction

Finding a Permanent Place for Permaculture

Beginning gardeners typically spend a lot of money on garden supplies. All of that mulch, fertilizer, and pesticides can burn a hole in anyone's wallet. But for those who utilize permaculture—their expenses are nearly non-existent. You could even say that the practice of permaculture is dirt cheap. But that's not to say that the dirt itself has no value. Quite contrary to the popular expression, have you ever considered how valuable the dirt beneath your feet really is?

It might sound like a funny question at first—but the soil that we trod upon and otherwise take for granted is a precious resource. I learned that early on in life, growing up on my parent's farm. I witnessed firsthand the joy of harvesting the first fruits of nature directly from the soil. In later years, however, I came to realize that as nice as the typical farm or garden may be, more often than not—the agricultural methods that were employed were not ideal for human health or the environment.

I've since taken a keen interest in understanding permaculture and how the natural environment can best be utilized for gardening. Rather than working against nature, like many other widely utilized methods of farming—permaculture makes the best of what nature already has in store. It cannot only provide a large yield of crops but also crops that are guaranteed to be both safe and delicious.

Organic foods, completely free of pesticides, can be allowed to flourish under the right permaculture conditions. I've personally grown hundreds of pounds of wholesome organic food. And the great thing about permaculture is that it can be successfully employed no matter how big or small the growing space for your garden is. Whether you intend to grow crops in a small space in your backyard or on a full-blown farm, specific eco-friendly techniques can be utilized to make the absolute best of it.

This eco-friendly technique allows one to naturally enrich the soil, eliminate weeds and other pests, and facilitate tremendous garden growth. I know it almost sounds too good to be true—but it's not. Honestly, it's just a simple matter of knowing what to do. Knowledge is power, right?

There is no need to overexert yourself with store-bought fertilizer, pesticides, and all of those other unnecessary additives. No matter what the sales rep at your local garden supply store might tell you—there is a better way!

Although we humans can often muddle up the process, nature does indeed follow a specific and efficient design. While the things that we do are often counterintuitive, unnecessarily wasteful, and strenuous, when nature is allowed to take its natural course—it all suddenly makes sense. Just take, for example, the common occurrence of leaves falling from trees.

If we were to see those leaves falling into our backyard, the natural inclination for most of us is to get out that trusty rake and scrape and bag all of those leaves up. Who wants a bunch of leaves around, right? By Spring, we'll have forgotten all about those bagged up leaves, however, and most likely we gardening fanatics will buy ourselves some mulch to put in our garden.

Yet, those fallen leaves we so callously cast aside are nature's very own mulch. The organic compounds of the leaves can break down in the soil and enrich it for further growth. That's not to say that anyone needs to leave their entire backyard covered in leaves, but saving a few bags to use as natural mulch come springtime would be a great idea.

These leaves can be shredded and then liberally sprinkled over garden beds in order to provide better insulation, aid in the retention of water, and generally keep soil from becoming too tightly compacted. Having a garden covered in leafy debris is natural. In their natural state, plants grow with all kinds of leafy debris around them as a beneficial part of their environment.

You see, it's really the contrived human notion of gardening through pristine, completely cleared-out garden beds, which creates some of the most common gardening problems. We keep the plant beds super neat and tidy before caking on store-bought mulch, fertilizer, and pesticides that do more harm than good.

Even if these methods seem to help in the short term—they are most likely doing long-term damage to the soil and general health of your crops. Quick fixes such as chemical pesticides, for example, have to be repeatedly administered in order for them to remain effective. Even worse, many insects and other pests can develop strong resistance to these chemicals over time.

This means that unless you are willing to continually up the ante and use even more powerful (not to mention more expensive) pesticides to knock these critters out—you are just wasting your time. Permaculture, on the other hand, is designed to create a permanent and sustainable agricultural environment for your crops. Instead of coming to your garden armed to the teeth with herbicides, pesticides, fungicides, and all those other awful, artificial *"cides"*— you should simply learn to work with what the natural environment already provides.

Even though much of modern agricultural production seems to have forgotten the importance of building up the naturally occurring permaculture—the ancients knew all about it. The ancient Incan Empire of Peru, for example, grew crops way up high in terraces, cutting right into the Andes mountains using all-natural methods.

At first glance, growing crops on a mountainside might seem a little impractical. But one thing the Incans didn't do, was haul huge amounts of artificial chemicals up with them. On the contrary, it was with the help of a hearty dose of guano (bird droppings) that they were able to naturally fertilize their crops wherever they took root. Guano is just about the richest kind of fertilizer one could use, and the Incas had explosive yields because of it.

But one must remember. Just because one method works well for one environment, it may not necessarily work the same for another. Permaculture is all about adjusting to the natural factors involved on the local level in order to create the right fit. And Florida, in particular, has a very unique bioregion that harbors a whole host of benefits for tremendous growth in a stable permaculture-oriented environment.

I wrote this book to specifically help those who would like to make the best of Florida's rich ecosystem. If done right, one could easily produce an abundance of fruits and vegetables all year round. Knowledge is indeed power. And now, I would like to impart that knowledge to you so that you can find your own unique garden growing niche. Your own permanent place in the Florida sun for an effective and sustainable food gardening permaculture.

What on Earth is a Permaculture Garden?

If you are reading this book, you have undoubtedly already heard that permaculture is beneficial for gardening. But such a superficial bit of reasoning only goes skin deep. In order to really appreciate what permaculture is and what it can do for your garden, a more in-depth understanding of its dynamics and how it works—is in order.

Permaculture, just as the wording of the term itself implies, is in reference to the imposition of a *permanent agriculture* of long-lasting and sustainable agricultural growth. Rather than temporarily scratching up the ground and heaping a whole bunch of artificial fertilizer, pesticides, and other chemicals onto the soil for a limited burst of growth—it seeks to take naturally occurring elements in the environment and use them to build a permanent backdrop of sustainability.

Instead of working against the natural elements on the ground —permaculture seeks to utilize them to their maximum extent. It's an intelligent, creative, and entirely innovative way to go about gardening—which uses planned wisdom rather than brute force to promote garden growth. The concerted efforts of an ecological garden, works for example, to establish fertile soil that is naturally resistant to weeds and yet also naturally facilitates tremendous growth of desired vegetation.

Sounds great, right? Well, two gentlemen by the names of David Holmgren and Bill Mollison certainly thought so. For it was Holmgren and Mollison who came up with the concept back in the 1970s. Although these two gentlemen are credited with establishing permaculture, in truth, they were simply reinventing the wheel. For the methods that they used were merely a recreation of what many ancient cultures all over the world had already been employing for centuries.

In that sense, we are not speaking so much of a new technique but rather a revitalization of a much older practice. Nevertheless, this newly revised version of an ancient method has the added benefit of keeping our more modern worldview in mind so that we can design the best type of permaculture garden for our current needs. For eco-friendly gardens are not necessarily one size fits all.

On the contrary, our personal gardening method will be the sum total of many possible parts. In order for it to succeed, it must be molded and shaped to meet your own individual needs. It's for this reason that it is often described as a kind of landscape "engineering." Every garden must be designed to meet very specific criteria for those who use it. Therefore, before we begin, we need to ask ourselves some very important questions.

IS PERMACULTURE A GOOD FIT FOR MY GARDEN?

Before you do anything else, one must ask themselves—*is permaculture gardening a good fit for me?* Will your immediate surroundings allow you to make the most of a naturally sustainable ecosystem? This gardening method is extremely adaptable, but nevertheless, some aspects of your garden space must be taken into consideration.

Such as:

- *General Ground Features*

Prior to attempting your own permaculture garden, it would be wise to consider some of the general conditions on the ground. Is the property on an incline? Or is it completely flat? Such things not only affect how deep you might dig but also how water flows on your property.

- *The Health of Your Soil*

Having healthy soil is key—but how does one gauge health? Well, for starters, your garden should have plenty of beneficial critters swirling around inside of it. Among the most obvious of these would be the ever loveable "earthworm." These worms are a tremendous help since they turn the soil and spread everything around, allowing for great circulation. But there are other organisms under the surface of your soil that are much smaller but just as important. Soil-based bacteria can be of tremendous help when it comes to breaking down the soil, as well as aiding in the conversion of nitrogen gas (plants love nitrogen!) in the plant's growth cycle. But you don't need to be a microbiologist or even have to whip out a microscope to know if there is healthy soil in your garden. For if you just know what to look for, there are some key giveaways that you can see with your very own eyes. Organically rich soil is darker than organically poor soil. It's also less packed together than nutrient poor-dirt. Organically rich soil, for example, tends to break apart more easily when you dig into it. A key test to how rich your soil is, involves poking a stick down into the ground and seeing how far you can easily push it before it gets stuck. If the soil is particularly poor you won't get very far, because the nutrient deficient soil will be too tightly packed together to push the stick down into it. If the soil is rich, however, the stick will slide right in there with relative ease. The aforementioned earthworms are also a good indicator since it is the earthworms themselves that secrete a whole hearty load of bacteria into the soil. You can always work to make your soil better, but if it's already in an extremely poor condition, you must keep in mind the amount of work that you would ultimately have to put in.

- *pH level of the soil*

The pH level of the soil is an indication of how acidic your soil may be. Most garden supply stores have pH test kits that you can buy over the counter. This usually involves strips that you place down into the soil. If, however, you do not have access to a store-bought pH test, there are more simplistic ways to do it. If your soil smells sour, for example—this would be another indication of particularly acidic soil. If, on the other hand, your soil is more alkaline in nature, it will tend to smell somewhat sweet. As you might imagine, smelling dirt is an imperfect science and takes some experience to be able to know the difference. Also, most of us probably have better things to do than smell the soil! Having that said, the best way to get an accurate reading of your soil's pH level is most likely through the use of the aforementioned store-bought pH test. These tests will give you a numeric read-out. Typically, a pH level reading between 6 and 7,5 is where you want your soil to be. For it is precisely within this range that soil has just the right level of both acidity and alkalinity to promote nutritious soil and promote growth. Another more DIY method would be to use baking soda and vinegar. This method requires you to dig down a few inches into the topsoil and put the soil into a clear container. Next, deposit just enough water to make the sample muddy and dump about a ½ cup of baking soda on top. Use a spoon or some other utensil to blend it all together. If you see foam and hear some fizz—this particular batch of soil is acidic. If, however, you do not happen to notice any such reaction, you can then whip out the vinegar. Repeat all of the afore-mentioned steps except, this time, use a ½ cup of vinegar instead of baking soda. If you notice fizz and foam from the vinegar, this is an indication that your soil is alkaline-based. Then again, if absolutely nothing happens, it's safe to say that your soil falls within the neutral range.

- *Existing Microclimates*

This book is focused on the climate of Florida but, even within a statewide climate, one might want to consider the even more specific "microclimates' ' that may be found therein. Just as the name implies—microclimates are a subcat-egory that falls within the more general climate makeup of a region. These microclimates could be affected by altitude, plant growth, and water deposits. Also, human-made struc-tures might affect the temperature, the distribution of sunlight and alter wind patterns. It's important to understand the specific factors influencing your particular microclimate before you start working on your permaculture garden. The more you understand what the factors involved are—the more easily you can tweak your garden design to make the best use of it.

- *Environmental Indicators from Nearby Plants*

Nearby, naturally growing plant life can tell you quite a bit about the local environment of your future ecological garden. These environmental markers are sometimes referred to as "indicator plants." Are the plants growing well—or do they seem particularly stressed? Are the plants thick-rooted? This could be an indication of compacted soil. Since thick roots are needed to push through densely compacted soil. These are just a few examples. Be aware of what mother nature is telling you.

- *Water Infiltration*

It probably goes without saying that water properly flowing down from the surface and into the soil is important for establishing a sustainable ecosystem. But how do you test the water flow of your soil?

It's actually fairly easy. Just scoop up some soil, push the dirt down into the jar and fill it up halfway. Now pour water on top of it. Mark how high the water is as it rests on the surface of the soil. Now, time just how long it takes for that surface resting water to be drawn down and absorbed into the soil. If it takes over an hour for it to absorb at least an inch of water— this is a sign that the soil is having issues with proper water infiltration.

- *Location of the Property's Utilities (Check Before you Dig!)*

If you know that you are going to be digging fairly deep, then you just might want to locate any utility lines that might be lurking underground. The last thing you need is to accidentally snip your cable, internet, or electric line. In most regions, you can call someone to come out and check them for you for free.

- *The Most Aesthetically Pleasing Arrangement for Your Property*

As practical as permaculture is, we can't help but want to make our arrangements as aesthetically pleasing as possible. Beauty really is in the eye of the beholder. Some may like to arrange their permaculture garden in traditional garden beds in the backyard. Others may prefer something entirely different. Perhaps the best arrangement for you would be one that integrates plant growth right up to your door. This could be done by weaving garden plots right alongside the walkway to your front or back door. Such aesthetics are completely up to you. It just depends on what you happen to consider the most beautiful at the time.

- *Your Ultimate Objectives for Your Permaculture Garden*

One of the most important things to consider is your ultimate objective in starting your garden in the first place. Why do you want an eco-friendly garden and what do you want to accomplish by establishing one? Would you like to grow food for yourself and your family? Would you like to grow enough to sell at a farmer's market? Or are you simply interested in growing plants as a hobby? Knowing your goals ahead of time is crucial for establishing just the right kind of ecosystem to meet your needs.

WHAT ARE THE ETHICS AND VALUES INVOLVED IN PERMACULTURE?

I'm sure we would all like to be ethical and have good values in life in general, but how does that translate to our ethics and values in permaculture in particular? First and foremost, someone who is an ethical permaculturist is one who is a good steward of the environment. That doesn't mean that you need to become some kind of hardcore environmentalist. It just means that you need to be mindful of your surroundings and consider how you affect the local environment as you establish your garden.

Permaculture is all about maintaining a good equilibrium with nature and the natural systems that are already in place. You don't want to make the environment worse than how you found it. You want to maximize what's already in place and do your best to make it better.

The exact opposite of the ethics and values prevalent in permaculture has been linked to someone carelessly plundering the Earth, as would be the case with a "strip mining" outfit, hellbent on sucking all resources out of a region and leaving nothing left in its wake. The ethics and values of permaculture, on the other hand, pride themselves in creating a sustainable environment that gives back even as it replenishes itself.

HOW CAN PERMACULTURE BENEFIT MY GARDEN?

There are many ways that permaculture can be of benefit. First of all—it can save you a whole lot of money. By using all-natural mulch, fertilizer, soil, and pest control methods, money that otherwise would have been spent at the garden supply store can be spent elsewhere. Using natural products also provides the benefit of not leaving waste behind.

Natural products gleaned from the environment will be used in their entirety without leaving any leftover junk. This is another great benefit in itself since such a method leaves the landscape pollution-free.

WHAT ARE THE 12 PRINCIPLES OF PERMACULTURE?

- *#1: Watch, Pay Attention, and Stay Involved*

If we aren't vigilant enough, we can overlook important aspects of the intricate ecosystem that we are trying to create. We need to take an active part in every aspect of the process from beginning to end. Permaculture is not something that you can just set up in one day and then forget about. You must be involved. This will allow us to make fully educated choices as we go about making a truly sustainable permaculture a reality.

- *#2: Capture and Conserve Energy*

For most of us, when we think of energy, we most likely think of the electric bill we pay at the end of the month and the gas that we (perhaps grudgingly) get from the pump. But there are more natural ways to capture and conserve energy. Harvested produce from your garden, for example, can be stored in a naturally dug root cellar which will keep them fresh and cool. Such a method saves tremendous energy since it does not require electric run, artificial refrigeration. Food can also be preserved through canning methods that do not actively consume energy, yet are able to keep food preserved for an astonishingly long period of time. Naturally harnessed energy can not only help you store your harvested crops, but it can also help you grow them. Greenhouses are designed to focus the light and heat of the sun directly down on crops, allowing them to utilize a maximum amount of energy even in colder temperatures. Since water is another important resource, smart capture and conservation techniques can be of tremendous benefit here as well.

- *#3: Reap a Good Harvest without Unnecessary Strain*

Another fundamental principle is to use smart and natural permaculture techniques to reap a good harvest without overly stressing the land in the process. If your objective is to grow just enough food for you and your household, appropriate measures should be taken to do so. If you wish to grow an even more abundant harvest with the purpose of selling the excess produce, this can effortlessly be done through natural methods as well.

- *#4: Regulate Your Actions and Learn to Adapt*

Those who practice permaculture need to learn how to regulate their own actions so that they are in sync with the local environment, as well as with what their garden needs. If your garden needs fertilizer, for example, rather than using store-bought chemicals, you can regulate materials found naturally in the environment to properly fertilize your garden. The same thing can be done for pest control through companion planting of certain crops that can ward off unwanted pests. You can easily learn to adapt to the local factors involved.

- *#5: Utilize Renewable Resources*

Another major principle of permaculture is the utilization of renewable resources whenever possible. The utilization of a renewable resource directly translates into the need to conserve rich and natural soil. Natural methods of turning the soil, such as crop rotation and the utilization of crop-friendly insects such as earthworms, for instance, are indeed a renewable resource that should be made use of on a regular basis.

- #6: Don't Be Wasteful

It is indeed a major principle of permaculture methodology to ensure that permaculture gardeners are not wasteful. You should live (if you choose to) by the philosophy that "everything has its use" and "everything has its purpose." The whole concept of a compost bin is the perfect demonstration of this kind of conservation at work since it takes what would otherwise be considered waste and transforms it into highly nutritious fertilizer. So don't let anything go to waste—just repurpose it and make use of it.

- #7: Follow the Patterns of Nature

Have you ever noticed that nature follows a pattern? It's true. Everything in nature seems to have been designed with a specific pattern in mind. It is an important principle, therefore, to consider these patterns and attempt to naturally follow them as best we can. Rather than completely tearing up the landscape that already exists and starting from scratch—we consider the natural flow of the surroundings and utilize them to build our garden in accord with it. Take into consideration the natural lay of the land, the condition of the pre-existing soil, and other factors of the local environment.

- #8: Practice Proper Plant Integration

The proper practice of plant integration is yet another important principle. For those that are not aware of just how important plant integration is, they just might be tempted to plant all of the same crops in one spot. For those who aren't experienced in permaculture, it would only seem logical to have a batch of all tomatoes here and a batch of all jalapeno peppers there. But when was the last time you saw a whole batch of anything naturally growing side by side in the wild? Nature isn't that neat and tidy. Nature doesn't isolate one group of plants from others. Typically, you find a wide variety of different plants growing among each other. And this natural design serves a purpose because these different types of plants glean different kinds of mutual benefits from each other and have learned to happily coexist as a result.

- *#9: Take Incremental Steps to Improve Your Garden*

In the fast-paced life of the modern world, we often want everything to happen as quickly as possible. But when it comes to having an ecological garden, it's always best to slow down the pace a little and take incremental steps to gradually improve your garden over time. The development of good and rich soil, for example, does not happen overnight. If you wish to abscond with permaculture and simply buy soil from the store—that's a different story. But if you wish to produce good soil naturally, it will take some time to do so.

- *#10: Variety is Good*

They say that variety is the spice of life. That's true. And it's also a great asset for your permaculture garden. Plants can bolster each other with mutual benefits when we learn to appropriately companion plant. It's also good to have a wide variety on hand just in case one specific kind of plant fails due to an unexpected disease or an infiltration of pests. That way, even if one certain type of plant is afflicted, the other plants are still going strong.

- *#11: Make Use of Every Inch of Space (Even the Edges)*

Permaculture is all about making the most of the space that we have. We should also respect the value of even the very edge of our garden, where our rich planting soil meets with other types of local environments. The edges can also be made quite productive by planting "heat-loving" plants such as grapes, beans, and squash right at the very edges of the garden beds. By building up these kinds of border plants at the boundary edge of your garden plots, you also provide extra protection and even shade to the rest of the plants. Even the very edge of your garden serves a purpose, so be sure to make use of it.

- *#12: Adapt to Change/Roll with the Punches*

Life is full of change and development. Has the temperature picked up? Rain suddenly increased? Are pests worse than usual this year? Don't get discouraged. If presented with an unexpected change, you should simply adapt your resources to meet the new challenges that you are presented with. You got this!

* * *

Permaculture gardening really does make use of the natural templates that nature provides so that we can maximize the resources already at our disposal. We've really just scratched the surface, but hopefully, what you have learned here will help you better begin your approach toward taking out your very own piece of the permaculture pie. With this baseline of understanding, in the following chapter, we will go over how to specifically design a permaculture ecosystem tailor-made to meet your needs.

READY, SET, DESIGN!

Do you want a perfect garden? One designed to your exact specifications? It's not as hard as it might seem. Once one becomes thoroughly familiar with the basic concepts of permaculture, it's just a matter of building upon this baseline of knowledge already established. With these concepts and principles in mind, we now need to go about bringing together the ingredients already readily available to us in nature. Once we do, we can then use these ingredients to shape and mold them into the exact kind of eco-friendly design we would like to create.

The design you use depends on your specific layout and exactly what you are trying to achieve. As mentioned earlier in this book, there is no one size fits all, but rather, various permaculture templates that can be pursued. Although the factors involved may vary, the central concept of building interconnected ecological systems for sustainability and growth will remain the same. There are, however, certain mainstays that you should be aware of when it comes to your approach—or *design tactics.* Let's go ahead and explore some of the most crucial of them now.

TACTICS FOR PERMACULTURE DESIGN

You may approach your permaculture project from a variety of different directions, but there are some concrete methodologies you might want to work with. Here are three design tactics you just might want to consider when going about your dream garden design.

3 Main Tactics for Permaculture Design:

- *Keep in Mind Your Mainframe Design*

In permaculture gardening, you should always begin with what is termed a "mainframe design." This is in reference to ascertaining the main aspects of the landscape and what will be specifically needed in order to begin the design process. Major factors involved in the mainframe design include: general access, artificial structures present, and the reliability of water. Let's consider the first of those mentioned—general access. This is in reference to just how accessible the property is and how easy it is to move about from one part of it to another. You want to make sure that it is well maintained and that there is nothing blocking access to the garden site. The property should not have any overgrown vegetation or other rubbish blocking common pathways. The garden should also be built away from natural hazards such as floodplains which would—predictably enough—block access during rainy seasons.

Along with access, we need to consider what artificial structures are present on a property and how they might affect your plans. You don't want to build your garden too close to an artificial structure, for example, that might potentially block out sunlight. Last but not least, when considering your mainframe design, you must keep the flow of water in mind. Does the water naturally flow downhill toward your garden, or is the water flow literally an uphill climb? Does your property have natural water deposits such as ponds or creeks? Does it rain consistently in your local environment, or do you need to find ways to conserve water in case of an excessively dry season? If so, you might want to consider ways of establishing natural irrigation techniques during times of drought.

- *Conduct a Sector Analysis*

If establishing a permaculture garden, you will need to conduct a sector analysis. Sector analysis entails taking a serious look at all external pressures in your local sector of the environment. External pressures from mother nature, or simply other factors beyond our control, such as the habits of a nearby neighbor. Natural pressures would be all of the likely culprits, such as sunshine, rainfall, wind, and local wildlife. Pressures from neighboring entities could include runoff from industrial facilities or even simply a residential neighbor with bad landscaping habits. As it pertains to natural pressures—during a sector analysis, we would need to take note of such things as wind patterns, the prevalence of rain, and the angles of sunshine during the various seasons. You might also want to keep in mind dry conditions that could potentially lead to wildfires. We would also be wise to take note of the most prevalent species of wildlife on the property. Are there a lot of herbivores present that might eat plants? Rodent-type animals such as gophers that could dig up your garden beds? This should be taken into consideration.

Regarding to non-nature external pressures inflicted by neighboring entities, are you downriver from an industrial facility? Is there a major interstate highway nearby? How about local residents? Does their behavior create any disturbances to the local environment? Short of complaining to the above-mentioned neighboring entities responsible for the disturbance, there is probably not much you could do about such interference directly. But once these issues have been identified in your sector analysis, you can at least do as much as possible to mitigate them.

- *Understand Permaculture Zones*

Starting at zero, there are actually 6 permaculture zones that need to be thoroughly understood for the purpose of permaculture. Like everything else in permaculture, these zones are interconnected and each one has an effect on all of the others. It's the understanding of what each permaculture zone is made of which allows successful integration of the working parts of your garden as a whole.

Before we get into all of the various zones, it's important to note that most permaculture gardens will likely fall within zones 0, 1, and 2. The zone that gets designated with a big fat "zero" is the most representative of "home and self." What does that mean? It means that zone zero represents our personal space—what we want and what we are comfortable with. Zone One is the zone that's immediately outside of your personal space. If you were to take a walk out your front or back door and take a few steps—you, my friend, are in Zone One. As you may have guessed, these permaculture zones move further and further – to the point that Zone Five is the furthest out. Understanding what falls under what zone can be useful when it comes to figuring out where you need to place things such as sheds, greenhouses, and fence lines. It could also help to figure out where and when to use irrigation.

Here's how your zoning might play out:

Zone Zero: Residence/Personal Space

Zone One: Nearby garden, where herbs, lettuce, and other regularly consumed veggies are grown.

Zone Two: A little further out in Zone Two, can be placed more intensive veggies such as kale, collards, and Swiss chard.

Zone Three: Further afield, more space can be allocated for more extensive and more robust crops, such as potatoes, tomatoes, corn, and the like.

Zone Four: Zone Four, on the very periphery of a property, where personal property and wilderness begin, one could grow mushrooms on old logs, squash, bundles of beans, and other similar types of plants. This semi-wild growth on the edge is sometimes labeled as being in the realm of "farm forestry."

Zone Five: Zone Five should be considered wilderness regions outside of the property, where only wild plant growth can be found.

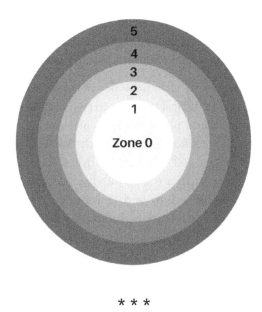

* * *

STACKING FUNCTIONS - HOW THEY CAN SAVE THE PLANET (AND YOUR TIME)

Putting agricultural layers together is a process known as stacking. This method seeks to maximize the potential of available resources and take advantage of them in the most effective and timely manner. In essence, stacking is an imitation of layering and multitasking, one can readily find already at work in the natural environment.

For example, in a forest, you have the canopy layer, the low tree layer, the shrub layer, the herb or herbaceous layer, the roots layer, the groundcover layer, vines, and an underlying fungal layer. Even if you love mushrooms, the word "fungus" might not sound too appealing, but the fungal layer of this stacked ecosystem is indeed essential. For not only could wild mushrooms take root, it is the fungal layer at the bottom of forest floor ecology that serves the purpose of reducing and getting rid of debris such as fallen logs, straw, woodchips, and other materials that might otherwise accumulate over time.

The opposite extreme from the bottom fungal layer is the canopy layer, which consists of the treetops or forest canopy. Here you might find places where animals such as squirrels and birds make their homes. Immediately below, you have the low tree layer where you'll find smaller fruit trees and/or dwarf fruit trees. This next layer is the shrub layer closer to the forest floor, where edible shrubs and fruit-bearing plants might reside. You then have a lower herbaceous layer with herb-type plants. The roots layer is underneath this, followed by the actual ground layer. Even lower is the aforementioned fungal layer.

As you can see, every layer in nature is stacked together and full of vital functions on every level. So how can we reproduce this sort of stacking with our permaculture garden? In the literal sense, you could utilize a stacked garden bed with multiple layers, but stacking is more than that. Making use of stacking functions could mean simply stacking one function upon another.

If you need to get rid of some weeds and recruit a few goats to eat up all of your weeds for you, and have the added benefit of the goats adding manure to the soil while their munching on plants—that my friends, is stacking. You've essentially stacked two functions together; weeding and fertilizing your soil simultaneously.

In old-school agricultural techniques, this form of stacked multi-tasking was quite common. If large quantities of wheat needed to be ground up in long-ago farming communities of yore, the locals would have a pretty simple solution. They would put all the grain on the floor of a big barn and hold a local barn dance! That way, folks could have fun stomping the wheat into oblivion while they danced the night away.

The following day, all the farmer would have to do was take a broom and sweep all of the ground grain up. Although such a thing seems downright comical, it would undoubtedly be much more fun (and a whole lot less time-consuming) than processing all that grain by yourself. So yes, stacking can be a literal, physical act of stacking layers of growth together in your garden, or it could simply be stacking different tasks/functions together in order to save yourself time and energy.

Here are a few more examples of how you might stack the functions of your garden:

- *Multi-Purpose Your Fruit Trees*

One of the great things about Florida is that the climate generally allows the growth of fruit trees. Folks can grow orange trees, grapefruit trees, and the like right out of their backyard. If you do indeed make fruit trees an integral part of your permaculture, then you should try your hand at stacking the functionality of those said trees and making them into multi-purpose producers. For as much fruit as these trees might provide, you can make them serve other beneficial purposes, such as positioning them to provide cool shade in the summer. They can also provide microclimates to other plants, a habitation for small critters, and even have them serve as a sort of privacy fence. Yes, rather than struggling to put down posts, pour cement, and nail fence pickets together, you could strategically plant some trees in just the right place, and you will have all the privacy and shade you could ever need! The trees will also provide crucial mulch since their fallen leaves are made up of nutrient-rich organic material. Trees require some maintenance, such as trimming and collecting fruit and the aforementioned leaves—but with minimal effort, you can indeed multi-purpose your fruit trees.

- *Develop a Diverse and Dense Landscape*

As it pertains to a permaculture garden, the more diverse and the denser your landscape is—the better. For the stacked functions therein will make for robust and healthy soil, rich in organic material, natural fertilizer, and healthy water flow.

- *Create a Forest Ecosystem aka Multi-Level Landscape*

By making use of a more literal interpretation of stacking, you can create multiple levels of growth through a forest-styled ecosystem. Grow trees that provide a natural canopy covering just like in the forest, and light and temperature-sensitive plants will benefit by being shielded from too much sun. The trees will also provide an essential base for climbing plants that otherwise would have difficulty growing without support. Using a tree as a natural base for climbing plants to wrap around, after all, certainly beats having to struggle with cumbersome stakes. Special herbs and shrubs growing nearby in the meantime will provide both a level of protection from pests and add nutrients to the soil.

- *Stack Your Water - How to Collect Rainwater*

Rain showers down precious water onto us for free. Therefore, we can stack the functionality of watering our plants by having the water naturally collected in a rain barrel, rainwater tank, or through the use of rainwater swales. The rain barrel method is probably the easiest to use of all of these options. It really is as simple as it sounds. All you have to do is get a sturdy barrel, set it outside, and wait for it to fill up with the rain. It doesn't matter if your barrel is wooden or plastic. Just make sure that its surface is clean. And if an actual barrel isn't available, you could always use buckets or some other similar container. Most tend to put their rain barrel near the edge of their roof or even under a gutter to collect the rain off, as the positioning of the barrel therein tends to help facilitate faster collection. Once your rain is collected, you will want to cover the top of the barrel with a lid in order to keep away water-loving insects such as mosquitos.

Besides rain barrels, another good option for rain collection is the use of rainwater tanks. Some are huge and made of stainless steel, while others are smaller and made from plastic or rubber. You might like steel for its durability, but rubber tanks are fairly versatile. Plastic is generally fine. But you must be mindful of any potential chemicals in the plastic that could seep into the rainwater. This usually isn't too much of a problem, but the possibility does exist. Much of the rest of your preference will be pure and simple aesthetics—what is most visually agreeable with the rest of your permaculture garden.

On the other hand, a permaculture swale is designed right into the landscape itself by way of a long ditch or trench dugout along the side of a slope in the land. Water collected in the swale can then be redirected to a nearby garden. Swales aren't for everyone, however, since the surrounding landscape or your property will dictate whether this particular form of water collection is feasible or not.

- *Chickens, Rabbits, and Goats to the rescue!*

Livestock such as chickens (and ducks), rabbits, and goats are great to have around. They can put a serious dent in pests since chickens and ducks eat plenty of bugs, and goats can eat up all of your weeds. These animals stack yet another functionality on top of all this by providing you with free fertilizer through their manure. They eat bad stuff like bugs and weeds and then poop out the good stuff to help your crops grow. You really can't beat it! The animals themselves also provide the stacked function of serving as meat if you choose to use them for that purpose.

* * *

HOW TO TRANSFORM A BARREN SOIL TO A HIGH YIELDING SOIL

Permaculture in the sunshine state is great, but one of the chief complaints is running into soil that is too sandy. After all, Florida is known for its beaches, so a little bit of sand mixture in certain soils shouldn't be all that surprising. But don't worry, for there are excellent strategies to transform that barren, sandy soil, into fertile, high yielding soil. So let's go over it now.

Compost! Compost! Compost!

If you are growing anything in Florida—compost is your best friend. The compost you create does not have to be anything too complex. All you need is just some regular old decaying organic material such as cut blades of grass, dead leaves, and other vegetation debris. You can also throw your banana peels and apple peels on top if you have them—since the remnants of fruits like these are great composter starters as well. Usually, compost takes a few months to get quickly into high gear, so you might want to start early if you go the traditional compost route. However, if you would like to speed things up a bit, you could engage in what's termed "hot composting." This method makes use of plant debris that are high in nitrogen and degrades (burns) faster than other materials. Just be wary of allowing any pests access to your biodegradable materials since pesky critters like mice just might want to take a spin in it! In order to prevent this, create practical barriers between your rich humus and any potential wildlife. Compost bins are designed with this in mind. At any rate, once your bins are secure, you can use your compost to turn that sandy soil into fertile and rich planting soil. This naturally made fertilizer will add crucial nutrients back to the earth and will aid in the retention of water. As good as it is for your garden, it's also suitable for general home maintenance since you can get rid of many waste products through composting.

So yes, by all means—Compost! Compost! Compost!

Manure, a Love Affair with the Soil

While manure might not seem loveable at first glance, once you mix it with your soil, these two elements are a match made in heaven. For, as any good gardener knows, manure can make or break the soil of a garden. The fact that manure is loaded with nitrogen can give any subsequent plant growth a tremendous boost. And as it pertains to Florida's sandy soil, we are in luck because this combination of nitrogen-rich manure and soil is just what we need to transform that sandy soil into a much more robust and moisture-retaining form of dirt. Manure will also have the effect of aiding the production of carbon, thereby providing even more energy and nutritious stimulus for your crops. Having that said, in a permaculture garden, it is of the utmost importance that the right kind of manure is used. There is a wide range of animal-based waste, but please be advised that household pets are usually not good candidates! Yes, just in case anyone might consider cleaning out their cat's litter box in their garden, it is crucial to know that cat and dog manure would be a bad addition. The type of waste product produced by these pets does not have the right balance of nutrients and is likely carrying parasites.

On the other hand, traditional animals produced manure from cows, goats, chickens, rabbits, and perhaps even horses would do the trick. Traditional manure such as this can be purchased, but in order to have truly sustainable permaculture, it would be best to have the manure-producing animal on the property itself. The easiest option for most medium-sized properties would be to have smaller animals such as goats, chickens, or rabbits do the work.

Cover Crops AKA Green Manure

Cover crops sometimes referred to as "green manure," are another great option when it comes to permaculture gardens in the great state of Florida. Cover crops serve as natural protective covers. They stand in the gap to prevent weeds from popping up. These valuable crops are also helpful for avoiding extremes in water runoff and help reduce erosion. They also provide needed shade during excessive heat so that the soil does not become too scorched in the hot Florida sun. All of these things are incredibly useful. But cover crops can have an even greater purpose. For this "green manure" can also serve as a source of rich, green-based fertilizer. It gives back valuable organic material to the soil, further enriching it and making it more fertile. Thick roots from plants such as radishes can also play a crucial role in turning and loosening up heavily compacted soil, thereby aiding in the overall texture of your garden's base.

Here are 9 types of cover crops that will prosper in Florida soil:

- *Buckwheat*

Buckwheat cover crops thrive in Florida and will transform into a rich, mulchy material that will help sustain neighboring plants after a couple of months. Buckwheat helps to take poor sandy soil and conditions it to be thicker and more capable of sustaining moisture. This cover crop is also great for blocking out weeds.

- *White Mustard*

This cover crop does well as the weather starts to get cooler. It may not be ideal for the hottest sections of Florida, but up in the FL panhandle, white mustard can thrive. The great thing about white mustard is that it carries a hearty dose of something called "glucosinolates." This compound works as a natural repellent for many pests and other harmful plant parasites. Mustard will eventually die out towards the winter, but if the remnants are left in place, it will come back once again as soon as springtime arrives. And in the meantime, the remnants of the old dying white mustard will serve as perfect "green manure" to further fertilize your garden.

- *Lupin*

Lupin is an eye-catching, purplish-blue plant with a lot of inherent benefits. But first and foremost, this legume-based plant is a nitrogen fixer, which essentially works as green manure on the plants it covers. So if you would like fast and abundant growth in your eco-friendly backyard, Lupin should be on your list.

- *Reversed Clover*

Clover is naturally rich in nitrogen and can add much fertility to your garden. It can also bring about a healthy dose of pollinating insects as the plant ripens. Clover is a hardy plant that can fill in the gaps in your gardens, covering up open spaces and preventing harmful weeds from growing.

- *Spinach*

Spinach is a hardy cover crop that does well in the later stages of the growing season. It doesn't take long for this nitrogen-rich plant to do its work. Spinach is indeed nutritious, and as it turns out, this leafy green plant is just as healthy for your soil as it is on your dinner plate.

- *Yellow Sweet Clover*

Sweet clover is another great nitrogen fixer. In Florida's climate, this hardy plant makes for a wonderful addition to your garden.

- *Red Clover*

Red Clover is excellent for Florida soil since it safeguards against erosion and greatly benefits the tilth of the soil. It also helps to push out any potential weed growth.

- *Marigold*

Marigold makes for a good cover crop because it contains a unique compound known as "alpha terthienyl." This powerful, protective compound can keep harmful bacteria, fungus, insects—and even viruses—at bay.

- Vetch

This cover crop is a durable, so-called "nitrogen fixer" that can do wonders to enrich the soil. Vetch should be planted right before winter sets in so that it can sprout up first thing in the Spring. Vetch is an early bloomer and by mid-spring is already shedding valuable, rich material that your garden will gladly utilize as a nutritious form of mulch for extra growth.

* * *

THE POWER OF EARTHWORM CASTINGS

Another great asset for permaculture gardening in Florida is the so-called "worm castings." The term "worm casting" is in reference to earthworm excrement. Earthworms themselves are naturally a great benefit to soil, simply because of how they move around and spread nutrients. But it's their waste products that can ramp up plant growth. This product is so crucial that folks even sometimes buy them in bulk from their local garden supply stores. Earthworm castings provide powerful nutrients, provide better aeration of the soil, and help facilitate healthy microorganisms in the soil. In addition, these castings can jumpstart seed germination. For best results, one should place ½ a cup of earthworm castings for every 100 sq feet of soil. They should be inserted just a few inches from the soil's surface.

* * *

Is No-Till a Good Idea?

If you happen to peruse any of the permaculture literature out there—it's not long before you might hear of a little something called "No-Till." So, what exactly is it—and will it be a good idea? As the name might imply, "No-Till" is a method employed that does not in any way stir up the soil. Even dead plants are not removed so that the soil can remain undisturbed. Dead plants can be trimmed, but they can not be pulled out by the roots. The No-Till strategy is permaculture at its finest since it gets us back to how things are done through nature. In the natural environment, there is no one there to till the soil as we humans do it, yet things still grow. So, is not tilling the soil actually a good idea? And is it worth doing? In some ways, yes. Because over-tilled soil can cause soil erosion and increase runoff. Tilling the soil breaks it down, and the more you till it, well—the more you have to till it! It's essentially a never-ending cycle. But if you just leave the soil alone and allow natural processes to take place and the natural ecosystem remains intact.

* * *

CAN MULCH MAKE FLORIDA'S SANDY SOIL FERTILE?

We've already touched on mulch a little bit in this book. We know that mulch is nothing more than a heavily concentrated amount of organic matter. In that sense, a pile of shredded leaves, dirt, and other plant debris would constitute a hearty helping of mulch. But it goes deeper than that. And as it pertains to how mulch can convert the sandiest of Florida soil to fertile growing grounds—it is the kind of mulch you use that can make the difference.

Consider the following four types of mulch:

- *Living Mulch*

Living mulch is an interesting concept. It entails the planting of a crop underneath another crop. It might seem strange to double up your yields like this, but it can be very beneficial. For example, let's say you're planting tomatoes and perhaps some oregano right below them. These two plants are natural companions and are mutually beneficial. The underlying plant will help prevent weed growth, aid in the retention of moisture, and draw in helpful critters to enhance the lives of both plants. This is the benefit of living mulch. This kind of mulch is also quite good for Florida-based weather since it thrives in humid, hot climates.

- *Chop and Drop Green Mulch*

Green mulch is similar to living mulch, except rather than the mulch being a living plant—it's from a recently living plant.

Green mulch does a great job of smothering out weeds and providing additional nutrients to the soil. And it's quite easy to apply. The use of this kind of mulch, in fact, is sometimes referenced as a "chop and drop." It's called such because all one really has to do is chop off the leafy material of just about any given plant and then drop it right on top of their garden soil. This fits in quite well with the minimalist nature of permaculture. Remember, permaculture is all about making gardening easier—not harder. Plants such as Parsley, Chives, Chickweed, Rhubarb, and even Dandelions are great candidates for chop and drop green mulch. But as it pertains to Florida's climate, in particular, the best candidates within your environmental reach would be: Comfrey; Pigeon pea; Fava bean; Lupin; Sunn hemp; Lemongrass; Vetiver; Swiss chard; Yarrow; Elderberry, and Nasturtium.

- *Fallen Leaf Mulch*

Leaf mulch is fantastic all year round, but in the fall season, many places receive an abundance of fallen leaves. Rather than trashing these leaves, one would be wise to collect them, shred them, and bag them. Fallen leaves make for some rather incredible mulch. Southern Florida might not be able to experience the seasonal change of falling leaves, but much of northern Florida does. So if your garden is in the panhandle especially, you should be able to make quite a bit of good use out of some good old-fashioned fallen leaf mulch.

- *Wood Chips*

Like fallen leaves, wood chips have a lot of dense biological materials locked within them that can be broken down into nutrients for plants. Neatly chipped, little pieces of wood that have been sitting around for several months are especially valuable since, at this point, they have already begun the process of decay.

* * *

The design stage of a permaculture garden is of tremendous importance. The steps and suggestions presented here do not have to be followed verbatim. But they should at least give you a basic idea as to the template that you will ultimately want to follow.

BIODIVERSITY IS KEY

SAY HELLO TO POLYCULTURE AND GUILD TREES

Biodiversity is important. And as it pertains to your permaculture garden, it is absolutely crucial. It is crucial because the more biodiversity your permaculture garden has, the better equipped it is to have more rapid and robust growth. It also equals more variety of nutrients available in the soil.

Biodiversity such as this is sometimes referred to as "Polyculture." The term is simply Latin for "Many" (Poly) and "Cultivations" (Culture). Yes, there are many different ways to cultivate your desired crops. It's fitting that ancient Latin is used to describe this ancient practice because polyculture methods have indeed been with us since the dawn of time.

It was the Native Americans of Central America and Mexico who made famous the so-called "three sisters" method of gardening, which involved a polyculture method of combining three different crops—corn, beans, and squash—in an entirely beneficial and supportive relationship.

The corn, first of all, provides the perfect structure for the beans to grow upon. Beans, by their nature, grow up on stalks that, if not given a structure to grow around, will fall and collapse as the plant becomes heavier. However, the corn stalk allows the bean plant to wrap around the corn stalk's base like a vine, giving the plant the support structure that it needs to grow in full health.

The beans provide a rich amount of nitrogen beneficial to the corn. The squash, in the meantime, planted nearby, on the ground by the bean and corn stalks, provides much-needed shade for the roots of the other plants so that they don't become overheated in the hot sun. This must have been particularly useful for farmers in the burning heat of Central America and Mexico.

In addition to all this, squash also serves as a natural repellent for many kinds of pests that are harmful to plants. It's unclear how exactly this combination was originally stumbled upon— but it works perfectly. And this is not the only polyculture combination that can provoke great success in plant growth. However, most modern cultivation methods utilize monocultures that are hellbent on growing just one crop in one plot of land at a time.

Just think of all of those fields where they grow nothing but wheat or nothing but corn. This is an unnatural, manufactured arrangement since nature, left to its own accord, would always allow for at least a little bit of biodiversity to be thrown into the mix. One of the significant downsides of those fields of monoculture, single file crops, is that they are often susceptible to being afflicted with massive swarms of opportunist pests.

For this reason, many modern farmers utilizing fields of monoculture crops are forced to use a ton of chemical pesticides on their plants.

Yet, if they would just find the right combination of companion crops in an integrated polyculture, they would be able to thwart most of those buggers the old-fashioned way. So, now that we've taken a look at what polyculture is and what it isn't—let's dive a little deeper into its benefits.

- *Better Pest Control*

There are a few reasons why plants might deter pests. For one thing, the plant might secrete chemical compounds that are unpleasant for particular pests and make them simply prefer to stay away. Another reason certain plants might ward off harmful bugs is that the plants actually attract natural predators that are harmful to those particular intrusive insects.

Imagine an invasive pest that loves tomatoes, being afraid to come anywhere near them because it's planted by a crop that attracts another critter such as a spider, that would love nothing better than to make a lunch out of that tomato munching bug. Such things are indeed possible when the right plant is put in the right place to ward off potentially harmful pests.

- *Improved and Richer Quality of Soil*

Having a variety of crops rooted in the soil can do wonders to improve and enrich your garden. By pairing plants with nitrogen fixers rich in much-needed nitrogen, you can significantly boost the nutritional value of the soil that your plants are growing in. In addition, producing a variety of plants fosters "nutrient cycling," in which valuable microorganisms are allowed to repeat their vital processes in a beneficial cycle.

- *More Abundant Harvest with Polyculture*

All of that rich nitrogen that polyculture provides most certainly doesn't go to waste. Plants grow bigger and faster when specially arranged nitrogen-rich plants are within reach.

- *You Better Your Odds with More Biodiversity*

Having a wide variety of plants is also beneficial due to the simple fact that it betters your odds should one particular crop fail. For example, a farmer growing nothing but cotton would be absolutely devastated if their crops were visited by a swarm of the dreaded cotton-eating boll weevil. Yet, if they had diversified their crops with several different plants—some of which being completely immune to this pest—their loss would be minimized, and their odds of success therefore would be increased.

* * *

Are There Any Downsides to Permaculture?

Considering all of these great benefits — are there any downsides?

One potential downside is the maintenance of polyculture, which requires frequent "mixing and broadcasting" of seeds, in order to thin out garden plots. This helps keep your garden space from getting too crowded with all of those companion plants. This does indeed require some vigilance on the gardener's part.

In addition to this, for some, a significant downside might simply be the struggle of trying to figure out which plant combinations work best for their particular polyculture arrangement. Admittedly enough, it can get a little confusing at times. But fortunately for us, there is a way to avoid this confusion—and it's through a little something called "Plant Guilds."

LEARN HOW TO MAXIMIZE YOUR OUTPUT WITH PLANT GUILDS!

In the old days of yore, folks used to be grouped together by their professions in categories that were referred to as "guilds." Just think of medieval guilds for stonemasons, carpenters, sailors, and the like. These working stiffs of the Middle Ages formed guilds to advertise their services better. Plant guilds are grouped together in a similar manner, with plants that fulfill a specific service or role lumped together in order to better understand which plant is suitable for what.

Crops that are particularly useful in warding off pests of plants with robust nitrogen are known for helping the community of plants they grow in. Therefore, these beneficial plants fall into what has been termed a "Community Function Guild." Having all of the various plants of a biosphere situated in specific guilds simplifies things tremendously.

It's like a master painter with several cans of paint to choose from. Within are various shades, but they serve the same similar purpose. That way, when the painter knows that they need blue, they pick up a can of blue paint. Or, as it were, when a polyculture planter knows that they need to ward off pests, they reach for the community function guild in order to do so

Another type of guild that you can use as your fast track to polyculture success is called a *mutual support guild*. The mutual support guild consists of plants that complement each other in mutually supportive ways such as a plant that needs nitrogen and a plant that needs to get rid of pests. This creates a mutually supportive environment.

Your mutual support guild will consist of all plant combinations that fit this bill. Another option is to make use of a little something called a "resource partitioning guild." These guilds host companion plants that are good at sharing responsibilities and resources. Such as a plant that provides cover and shade to a rooted smaller plant that's great at conserving moisture.

An example of this would be a Pecan tree, with several rhizome/underground plants, such as radishes and carrots, arranged around the tree bottom. The Pecan tree provides shade, while the radishes and carrots break up the soil and conserve moisture.

But as it pertains to your permaculture garden in Florida, one of the best and most productive guilds you could ever fashion are the fruit tree guilds. We will explore all the various combinations of fruit tree guilds in the next section.

FLORIDA'S FRUIT TREE GUILDS

Florida is known for its fruit. Oranges are iconic with the state. And I'm guessing you wouldn't mind being able to harvest an abundance of fruit in your garden. One of the best ways to go about doing that is to make use of a little something called fruit tree guilds. So, what exactly is a fruit tree guild? What do they consist of, and how exactly can they be of benefit?

Fruit tree guilds, just like any other polyculture guild, seek to place fruit trees in beneficial companion planted arrangements that will allow them to best realize their potential and facilitate healthy growth. Fruit tree guilds typically focus on creating a unique plant ecosystem that centers around one fruit tree. The fruit tree is the centerpiece with a biodiverse range of plant satellites around it, which compliments and mutually benefits the fruit tree and each other.

These helpful little satellites are often referred to as "under-plantings" since they are generally planted around and under the fruit tree. These supportive underlings of the fruit tree can work as nitrogen boosters, pest deterrents and even serve as mulch as they drop leafy greens around the roots of the fruit tree.

Creating such a long-lasting, and sustainable permaculture by way of a fruit tree guild is of incredible benefit. But it will take a little bit of time and effort in order to make sure that you do it right. You also have to make sure that you build a fruit tree guild that is appropriate for the amount of space you have to work with.

If you have more than a couple of acres of land, you probably don't have anything to worry about. Someone with 2 or 3 acres could build a relatively extensive and elaborate ecosystem for their fruit tree guild. But if you have only half an acre of land to work with, on the other hand, you might have to be a little more conservative. You may even want to consider using a smaller tree such as a so-called "dwarf fruit tree" or perhaps just some centralized bushes of bramble berries.

At any rate, whatever type of fruit tree (or bush) you choose, this will be the centerpiece of your fruit tree guild from which all of your other carefully selected polyculture crops will spiral out from.

Here's how a typical fruit tree guild might work. First, you would have the fruit tree itself as the aforementioned center or "anchor" of the guild. Then, a supporting cast of characters planted around it comes from here on out. These could include any of the following: cranberry, blackberry, gooseberry, beetroot, nasturtiums, sunflowers, dandelions, marigolds, radishes, clover, carrots, oregano, sage, beetroot, and onions. These are mostly a variety of shrubs and herbaceous plants.

It would look a little something like this:

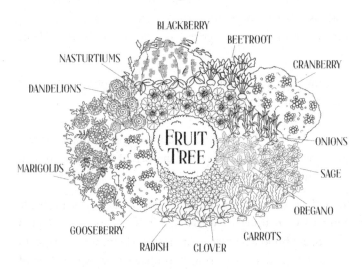

A Fruit Tree and Its Satellites

Layers	Plants			
Shrub	Oregano: medicinal, pest deterrent	Blackberry: good mulch, nitrogen fixer, pollinator	Gooseberries: good mulch, nitrogen fixer, pollinator	Cranberry : good mulch, nitrogen fixer, pollinator
Herb	Onions: medicinal, pest deterrent	Sage: medicinal, pest deterrent	Marigolds: medicinal, pest deterrent, pollinator and weed suppressor	Dandelions: medicinal, pollinator
Climber	Nasturtiums: pest deterrent, pollinator, weed suppressor and insulates the soil			
Groundcover	Clover: medicinal, weed suppressor, nitrogen fixer			
Rhizome/ Underground	Carrots: weed suppressor, loosen soil	Radish: pest deterrent	Beetroot: medicinal, natural dye	

Regardless of the type of fruit tree you are growing, this anchor crop would be surrounded by beneficial shrubs, herbs, a couple of rhizome plants, and a good groundcover. As for our shrubs; oregano, blackberry, gooseberries, and cranberry —all of these shrubs are good for attracting beneficial pollinating insects, and birds and provide suitable protection from the wind. Oregano also provides the added bonus of being a great pest deterrent.

Herbs planted near the roots of the tree, such as onions and sage, are powerful pest deterrents as well. Marigolds and dandelions, in the meantime, are known as "dynamic accumulators," which sink deep roots that bring up the best minerals and nutrients in the soil. Our climber plant Nasturtiums also plays a crucial role, since it's an excellent weed blocker, as well as a great soil insulator.

Our resident rhizome crops—carrots and radish—are also important because they help break up compacted soil. Our lone groundcover crop, clover, on the other hand, is an excellent nitrogen fixer, sustaining our whole tree ecosystem with a hearty supply of nitrogen.

Now here's another example of a potential Fruit Tree Guild that would make a great addition to your garden:

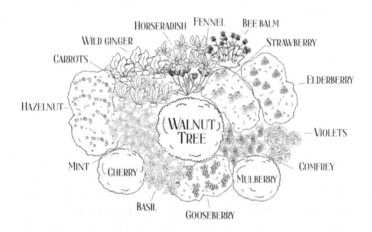

A Walnut Tree and Its Satellites

Layers	Plants			
Sub Canopy	Cherry	Mulberry		
Shrub	Hazelnut	Elderberry	Gooseberry	
Herb	Fennel	Comfrey	Basil	Bee Balm
Groundcover	Mint	Strawberries	Violets	
Rhizome/ Underground	Carrots	Horseradish	Wild Ginger	

You may have noticed that the example above has an additional category of supportive plants entitled "sub-canopy." Canopy is a term in reference to being treetop level. In this Fruit Tree Guild arrangement, the towering walnut tree is this ecosystem's canopy/upper level. Below this tall tree, however, smaller growth trees such as cherry trees and mulberry trees can be placed directly underneath to render support at the "sub-canopy" level.

Beneath the sub-canopy are the shrubs that attract pollinating insects and serve as a buffer against strong winds. Herbs such as basil, fennel, comfrey, and bee balm can be arranged one level below the sub-canopy, where they can work as pest deterrents as well as nitrogen fixers. In addition, fennel is a great antifungal agent, which is vital since fruit-bearing plants are often plagued with fungal outbreaks.

Comfrey also provides plenty of green manure mulch. In the meantime, groundcovers such as mint, strawberries, and violets work as additional pollinator attractors. Just as was the case with the previous arrangement, this Walnut Tree Guild also has hearty Rhizome/Underground plants such as Carrots, Horseradish, and Wild Ginger planted near the tree so that their powerful roots can help break up the soil, ensuring that it will not become too compacted.

Now with the aforementioned two templates in mind, let's go ahead and walk you through how you would construct a fruit guild of your own. First of all, find plenty of space where you can plant your tree. Then, as you plant your tree, you always want to make sure that you point the roots in a downward position. Because if you are not careful and you accidentally get them to point upwards—your tree will become more susceptible to plant-borne illness.

Another good tip to keep in mind when digging a hole to drop the tree into be sure to keep that same dirt you're digging handy. Don't lose track of your soil because you will need it to fill the hole you just dug! It might sound like common sense, but plenty of would-be tree planters have accidentally tossed good soil to the side, only to realize they need it to cover their tree.

And if your dirt does get tossed, and you find yourself coming up short, please avoid using any store-bought soil. Because for this task, only your healthy soil from the immediate area of the dig site will do. So yes, make sure to keep a neat pile of your freshly dug dirt nearby so that it won't be hard to put it right back in place once your tree is securely inserted down into the ground.

And when packing the soil back over the hole, you want to be mindful to keep everything as uniform as possible so that you can avoid any air pockets forming later. With your tree planted into the ground, the next thing you want to look out for is any grass encroaching on the dig site. Pull away nearby grass, and most certainly get rid of any weeds that are near the tree so that the tree will get a good start in its life cycle without having to battle grass and weeds for precious resources.

You might also want to put some compost and perhaps a little bit of mulch around the freshly planted tree to help boost its growth. A few gallons worth of shredded leaves and chopped-up wood chips spread around the base of the tree can really do wonders when it comes to giving this tree a healthy start. After all of these preliminary measures have been taken care of, you will want to literally stake out your territory.

Place some sticks, stakes, posts, or what have you—in a circular arrangement around the tree to establish what is termed a "drip line." This basic perimeter is established as a gauge for how far the roots of your tree will grow. You want to have enough room for your tree's roots to grow unhindered, so make sure that you measure out a perimeter far enough out for them to do so.

You also want to ensure that the soil within your drip line perimeter is as healthy as possible. With all of these things established, you can consider what kind of companion plants you might want around your tree. We've already laid out some basic examples, and there is most certainly a wide variety to choose from. But to break it all down, there are generally 7 types of plants that you will ultimately want to have around your tree.

These 7 plant types should be able to:

- Serve as a pollinator attractor
- Serve as a barrier to invasive wildlife
- Work as an aid in fertilizing the soil
- Provide natural mulch
- Create nectar for pollinating insects
- Suppress pests
- Prevent grass overgrowth

Another good tip for starting your own fruit tree guild is to start it off in the Fall. Unless you live in the southern tip of Florida, most of the state does indeed have a noticeable cooling in the Fall season. It should be during this cooler time of year that you should plant your fruit tree; that way, it will begin sprouting up just in time by early Spring.

And in the Florida climate, in particular, trees are well suited for being planted in the Fall because of the hot summers and relatively mild winters.

In the sunshine state, the ground does not get too cold until December, and after a very brief freeze, Spring is well on the way. It's better to plant in the Fall in Florida and let the plant overwinter because it allows the budding plant to avoid the excessive heat and potentially dry weather of Florida in the late summer. By planting after summer, the roots are able to develop in a relatively mild and stable environment. Therefore, the tree will have a solid base to grow strong with the first rays of Spring.

Furthermore, the Fall season is more in line with the natural cycle of the fruit tree. Most trees, after all, drop their leaves in the Fall and go dormant in winter. They also drop seedlings that can begin to grow roots and sprout up as brand-new trees in the Spring. Heck, even squirrels bury their nuts right before winter, and if that furry squirrel forgets to dig up later—that nut could very well become a new tree as well! At any rate, as it pertains to permaculture in Florida, Fall is indeed the perfect time to plant.

Here are some more amazing Fruit Trees from which Guilds could be made:

- Almond Trees
- Apple Trees (North and Central Florida)
- Avocado Trees

- Black Locust Trees
- Carambola Trees
- Cherry Trees
- Chestnut Trees
- Date Palm Trees
- Elderberry Trees
- Feijoa Trees (Cold-hardy and durable—Grown in North and Central Florida)
- Fig Trees
- Guava Tree
- Jujube Tree (Chinese Date Tree)
- Loquat Tree
- Macadamia Tree (Grows in Central and South Florida)
- Mango Tree
- Mulberry Tree
- Olive Tree (Ideally Central Florida and Tampa Bay)
- Papaya Tree
- Pawpaw Tree
- Pear Tree (North and Certain Parts of Central Florida)
- Pecan Tree
- Plum Tree
- Pomegranate Tree
- Silver Birch Tree

* * *

PLANT FUNCTIONS IN GUILDS

Go wild with plant guilds! Knowing the role that each plant fulfills in your garden will make your job much easier:

Nitrogen fixers:	Cowpeas
Each of these plants (roots) are colonized by microorganisms that will extract nitrogen from the air and supply it to the plants around	Spurred butterfly pea
	Fava beans
	Green beans
	Pigeon peas
	Lupins

Dynamic accumulating AKA Companion planting:	Peppers	Basil and Onions
Not only they can improve soil quality and provide shelter to one another (from wind and too much sun), but they can also attract beneficial bugs for pollination.	Carrots	Beans, Garden peas, Onions, Tomatoes and Lettuce
	Sweet corn	Cucumbers; Garden peas, Beans, Melons, Potatoes, and Squash
The plants on the left column thrive amazingly well alongside each plant on the right column	Garlic	Beets, Corn, Carrots, Radishes, Eggplant, Spinach, Peppers, Cucumbers and Tomatoes

Repellers:	Basil
Repels nematodes, insects and many other pests	Lavender - *Phenomenal* lavender can tolerate the climate of Florida
	Lemon grass
	Lemon thyme
	Mint
	Rosemary - It may need to be protected from freezes in colder areas of the state
	Sage
	Catnip

Mulchers:	Comfrey
These plants can be used as natural fertilizer	Jerusalem artichokes
	Clover
	Nitrogen fixing trees/shrubs

Suppressors:	Squash
Suppresses weed growth	Pumpkin
	Nasturtiums
	Mint
	Strawberries (Camarosa and Festival grow well in Florida)
	Pennyroyal
	Thyme

* * *

OTHER EXTRAORDINARY PLANT GUILDS

So far in this chapter we've focused on tree guilds—but what about other plant guilds? The basic definition of a plant guild, after all, is just an assorted group of crops that live in harmony with one another. Each member of the guild plays a role to help the entire group. Having that said, what other kinds of plant guilds are there? And what do they have to offer?

- *Tomato Guild*

Just like a tree guild, the tomato guild has an anchor crop— the tomato—around which all the other plants in the guild revolve. The tomato anchor is surrounded by supporting groundcover plants such as basil and arugula. Basil is great for deterring harmful pests, whereas the arugula does double-time attracting beneficial pollinators. Further out from the anchor, we can plant useful herbs and shrubs such as onions, marigolds, and borage. Onions have deep roots and are therefore great at loosening up the soil, whereas borage sprouts up as a good barrier against the wind. Marigolds in the meantime are great for further pest deterrence, even while serving as a magnet for pollinating insects.

- *Corn Guild*

Corn can be used as a guild anchor, with the classic climbing plant beans growing up around the corn stalk. The beans in turn provide plenty of nitrogen to enrich the soil. Squash is then placed around the corn stalk to provide sufficient ground cover, and to help retain moisture in the soil.

- *Banana Guild*

Even though bananas are often thought to grow on trees—the plant that bananas come from is technically not a tree at all. Bananas grow on a large, thick stalk. Nevertheless, the banana plant can indeed serve as an anchor for a guild. The banana crop is great for providing shade, protection from wind, and retention of moisture for other surrounding plants. Sweet potatoes would provide a good groundcover for this guild. Lemongrass can be planted as a deterrent to weeds. Jackfruit can also be planted nearby for an additional source of nitrogen.

* * *

PERENNIALS VS. ANNUALS

What are Annuals?

As the term might imply, a plant categorized as an "annual" is a crop that blooms only on an annual basis. This means that it blooms once a year, and then at the end of that growing season, it dies. This is the end of the road for this short-lived crop. Many low to the ground crops such as flowers, weeds, and vegetables fall into this category. These plants grow quickly for a season and then drop seeds right before they die off so that the cycle can be repeated with a brand-new annual plant.

In order for such plants to have rapid growth, they often need a lot of fertilizer, making their upkeep and maintenance more difficult. Furthermore, since the plant life of these annuals is so brief, their root structures are relatively limited. After all, they are only around for a short season, so they quite literally do not get the chance to put down deep roots. As such, these crops are not reliable partners as it pertains to soil stabilization. If a companion plant is necessary for this purpose, a perennial crop would be a more logical choice.

What Are Perennials?

Unlike annuals, perennial crops are in it for the long haul. Perennial plants do not disappear at the end of a single growing season; they stick around for several. Since trees are technically considered perennials, it could be said that some even live for hundreds of years. Considering their long life, these perennials grow much more slowly than annuals. As such, they have time to put down extensive root systems into the soil. These plants are built to last, and the general sturdiness of their overall structure is a clear testament to that fact.

Their deep roots allow perennials to have much better access to important nutrients lodged deep underground. These roots grow as the plant is searching for water and food, and at the same time, create the added benefit of stabilizing the surrounding soil and establishing a bulwark against soil erosion. If you want to save yourself some work, changing your annual garden to a perennial one would be advisable.

Here are some of my favorite perennial crops that prosper in Florida:

- Comfrey
- Creeping thyme
- Lavender
- Rosemary
- Yacon
- Jerusalem artichoke
- Egyptian walking onions
- Wild black cherry
- Ground cherry
- Sweet potato

* * *

NOW THAT YOU KNOW YOUR TREES—KNOW YOUR ZONES

As you might have noticed from earlier lessons in permaculture—much of the permaculture landscape can be sectioned off into various compartments. And when we consider establishing our fruit tree guilds, we would be wise to consider certain zones of operation. These zones entail specific habitats and environments in the Florida landscape.

The United States of America as a whole is blessed with a wide range of temperatures. From frigid cold to scorching hot—and just about everything you could imagine in between. And thanks to the folks down at the United States Department of Agriculture (USDA), all of these unique hot and cold zones have been mapped out and divided up into specific zones. There are 13 zones in total, with a variety of sub-zones.

Knowing these zones and what kinds of temperatures they offer helps you better understand what you will need to make any permaculture garden found therein successful. The scale begins with 1A, where locales like frigid Yukon, Alaska, clock in as the coldest, and it gets warmer as the number increases.

For the permaculture climate in Florida—the following zones are of prime interest:

- Zone 8: From Pensacola to High Springs
- Zone 9 A: From Jacksonville to Gainesville and Ocala
- Zone 9 B: From Orlando to Tampa and Lake Okeechobee
- Zone 10 A: From Fort Myers to Naples and Vero Beach
- Zone 10 B: West Palm Beach to Fort Lauderdale and Miami
- Zone 11 A: Florida Keys

As just a cursory glance at these stats might indicate, the Pensacola/High Springs region up in the Florida panhandle is the coolest part of the state. It ranks as a zone 8 and its cooler temps would only make sense since it is indeed in the northern reaches of Florida. Now, if we were to go way down to the tip of Florida, near Miami, we would find ourselves locked into hot tropical temps that reach all the way to a classification of being Zone 10 B.

And even further out, south of the Florida peninsula entirely, around the island chain known as the "Florida Keys" we find things getting even hotter. This region ranks as a scorching hot Zone 11—the hottest and most humid part of the entire state of Florida.

But hot weather is not conducive to some other crops, such as apple trees, which tend to enjoy cooler temperatures. So if the sun is a little too hot for certain types of trees, you can also mitigate the effects of the heat through some of the aforementioned fruit tree guild arrangements. Specifically speaking, shrub growth arranged around the base of a tree can provide a shady, cooling effect for that entire section of your garden.

* * *

THE AGE-OLD QUESTION—HOW FAR APART SHOULD TREES BE PLANTED?

If you are planting more than one fruit tree in your fruit tree guild, one of the biggest questions you might need an answer to is—how far apart should your trees be planted? You most certainly do not want to plant them too close.

As mentioned earlier in this chapter, one of the reasons you do a drip line and create an established perimeter is to ensure your tree has ample space. But like all things in life, sometimes things can get a little complicated as you plant multiple trees, and even the best drip lines can become a bit blurred as trees grow and expand their reach. That's why it's important to have at least a rough understanding of how big your trees might grow before you plant them side by side.

Experience, after all, is the best teacher, and tree planters have a long history to draw upon for how big these trees get. Fig trees, for example, are known to generally do well when they are placed about 15 feet apart from each other. Peach and Lychee trees, on the other hand, need more room—around 20 feet. And if you have your heart set on planting Jackfruit trees, these fruit-bearing behemoths could require as much as 30 feet between them.

However, for those of you with more limited space, don't' be discouraged, for there are plenty of good so-called "dwarf trees" which can grow the same exact fruit, taking up much less space. Dwarf apricot trees, for example, will only need around 8 to 10 feet between each other. So, how far apart should your trees be planted?

WHAT'S THE BEST PLANT POSITIONING?

It's a known fact that trees love the sun (just as much as we humans love the shade that trees provide,) so it goes without saying that you will want to position your tree so that it has plenty of sun. Having that said, however, there are a few things you might want to keep in mind. You should be careful if planting your tree too close to nearby structures. You wouldn't want your tree, for example, to grow too close to a neighbor's fence.

Perhaps the backyard corner seems like the perfect spot, with the sun streaming down on your tree and a perfect view for you—but if the tree's limbs are reaching over onto someone else's property, this could create a major headache in the future. Your neighbor could become agitated as leaves, tree limbs, and perhaps fruit falls down on their property. Maybe you thought you would both benefit from that mango tree—but unfortunately (and I don't know how this is even possible), not everyone is a fan of mangoes! But if you have your heart set on having that tree in that specific corner of your backyard, consider talking with your neighbor first. They may actually love the idea of reaping the rewards of having a mango tree with just half of the workload.

In order to avoid all of this, you would be best suited to plant your tree in a more centralized location so that it won't affect your neighbors. You also want to position it away from your house and other underlying structures. Some trees, after all, can develop some rather strong and sturdy roots that run deep and far into the ground.

And the last thing that you need is a tree with roots that might disrupt underlying foundations—or even underground pipes and sewer lines.

So in order to keep away from sudden catastrophe, and if you're not aware of any pipes that run under the foundations of your house, **call 811**. It is the national call-before-you-dig phone number.

OH, HOW WILL POLLINATION WORK?

There are many would-be fruit tree planters who might forget that these trees need pollination! Some trees are self-pollinating and you won't have to worry about them too much—but not all of them. For this reason, fruit tree guilds might be so important since you can underplant them with companion crops that attract pollinating insects.

Otherwise, you could always simply plant more than one tree so that they can help provide pollination to each other. That way when the trees are ready to begin the blooming process, they can send pollen back and forth to each other in a mutually supportive system. This pollination will help to stimulate the production of fruit.

* * *

As you can see—biodiversity is crucial to the creation of a long-lasting and sustainable ecosystem for your garden. And as this chapter has shown, polyculture and strategically planted guilds can make all of the difference in the world. Each plant has a unique purpose that it can fulfill when arranged appropriately. It's only when they come together that these crops truly reach their fullest potential. We can then really begin to appreciate the beautiful harmony of their growth and development.

How to Make Your Suburban Backyard A Winner!

Are you a little tight on space? Is your suburban backyard not the biggest one on the block? Well, don't fret! We've got the solution for you. Believe me, I know full well that one of the biggest reasons many budding backyard gardeners get discouraged is due to the simple fact that they think that their yards are too small.

Because when you get right down to it—it really is just a matter of perception. You may look out at your yard and think to yourself, "Wow—my yard is too small to plant all the foods I'd like. This will never work! I shouldn't even start!" But looks can be deceiving. For even in the tightest of spaces, you can find innovative means to let the little room you have, provide the best garden for your personal needs. Let's go over a few of them now.

SAVING SPACE AND SAVING FACE WITH RAISED GARDEN BEDS

Raised garden beds are a classic solution to limited space and are typically a perfect methodology in Florida's unique climate. There are a few reasons for this. Number one, it helps to improve the soil. It does this by raising the soil above ground level and then enclosing it in a box-shaped frame.

This frame is commonly constructed of wood, although bricks, stones, and other materials might be used as well. I like to use simple 2 by 4 pieces of wood that can be neatly placed around the garden bed as a surrounding frame. This surrounding structure helps provide extra support—and more importantly—aids in the prevention of soil erosion.

Let's take a closer look at the main benefits that raised garden beds provide:

- *Better Soil Conditions*

The soil quality is always important, but in Florida, one must really take care. Florida has some rather sandy soil, after all. And sandy soil is not exactly the most fertile on its own. This can be corrected by placing a concentrated amount of gardening soil mixed with compost materials, placed inside the supportive structure of a raised garden bed. The protection of the raised bed keeps traffic away from the growing area. This prevents the trampling of your plants and keeps the soil from getting too compacted. This less compacted soil will provide better water and airflow, which will translate into a better garden foundation.

- *Bigger Yields*

Raised garden beds can provide bigger yields because crops can be planted closer together and in more significant quantities. The raised platform can also reduce plant damage by keeping harmful critters such as nematodes away from the roots of your crops.

- *Annual Crop Rotation*

A great benefit and methodology entailed with raised garden beds is the ability to engage in annual crop rotation. Good soil is hard to come by and shouldn't go to waste. It's like keeping the seat warm for the new guy—because each crop you rotate will be able to take advantage of the nutrient soil that the previous crop left behind. By changing up our variety of crops and alternating them with different kinds, we also keep potential pests and predators off balance. If you have tomatoes in place one season and then plant basil in the same spot the next—those little buggers will find it hard to keep up. The variety of crops you rotate will also provide many added benefits to each of the plants involved. If, for example, you keep four basic plants in rotation, such as : legumes, nightshades, and roots—you can reap a whole host of mutually beneficial rewards. The legumes (beans) are nitrogen fixers, so plant them first to build up the soil. Next, you can rotate this crop with a good nightshade plant such as tomatoes that absolutely love this nitrogen-rich soil. Finally, rotate the nightshade/tomatoes with a good root-based plant such as carrots. These plants will grow deep down, seeking nutrients, further breaking up the soil as they go. After this, rotate back to your legumes, and this cycle can be repeated indefinitely. Other combinations could have you plant your tomatoes first, then your beans, and then your carrots. But whichever sequence you choose, these plants still provide the same benefits to each other if rotated regularly.

- *Better Access and Less Maintenance*

At first glance, the better access allowed by a raised garden bed may seem like a minor benefit—but it's not. Just think of those times you've had to kneel and bend over attempting to take care of low to the ground, and inconveniently planted crops. Simply by raising your garden beds, you can avoid this nuisance and make the maintenance of your crops much more accessible. They also reduce the level of care involved. Close planting within the raised beds prevents weeds. Frames also provide less worry about pests since it's not hard to wrap chicken wire around the wooden frames, eliminating many intrusive little garden munchers such as rabbits, chipmunks, birds, and the like. That way, you have perfect access, but those critters do not. Better access, less worry, and less maintenance. It certainly beats running outside every few minutes waving a stick!

4 TYPES OF RAISED GARDEN BEDS

1. ***Rectangular raised bed*** *(step-by-step guide)*

- Collect all the materials you'll need

-Around 4 logs from your nearby forest (or if you have a stump in your garden, chop it up more and use the wood pieces instead)

-Assemble 2 buckets of branches from the same forest
-Chipped wood from your local supplier
-A mix of soil made of ⅓ of sand, ⅓ of clay, and ⅓ of forest humus (another mix of soil that you can use is ⅓ of manure compost, ⅓ of sawdust, and ⅓ of worm castings)
-You can use wood planks (8ft by 4ft) or natural stone for the "frame" of the raised bed (you can also use bricks, fallen logs, straw bales, or even concrete blocks)

- Now assemble!

-Build the frame in your desired gardening space
-Place the logs inside as the base — Tip: you can also use cardboard as the first layer if you have a lawn. It will prevent the grass from getting into your garden soil
-Fill the space around the logs with the twigs and branches collected from the forest. Cover the logs as well
-Cover it with around 4 inches of chipped wood
-Create the 3 soil mixture and add 5 or 5 and a half inches to the raised bed
-Finally, top it all up with more chipped wood (around ½ inches)

- It's time to plant all your desired veggies

-Plant your seedlings
-And now it's a waiting game!

Tip: The plants that you can easily grow in raised beds are every companion plant your heart desires!

2. *Herb Spiral*

"The spiral is the most efficient way of storing things and saving space. The herb spiral can fit a large amount of growing bedding in a compact structure that is easy to fit outside your kitchen door."

— -ADRIAN BUCKLEY

Just as the name might imply—herb spiral garden beds are shaped in spiral form, with its spiral arms stretching out several feet from its center. This plant's design is just as strategic as it is aesthetic. It's strategic because crops are purposefully planted within the spiral arms according to their particular needs. Plants that are in need of plenty of sun are positioned to make the most of sunshine, whereas plants that like shade are placed to make the most of shadier conditions. Some spots in the spiral arm may also be more conducive to water-loving plants, while other locales within the herb spiral are the perfect place for plants that thrive in more dry environments.

Benefits that Herb Spirals Provide:

- Bigger Yield of Crops
- Greater Variety of Crops
- Microclimates

- Healthier Crops
- Aesthetically Pleasing Arrangement
- Good Even Over Concrete
- Easy Access and Maintenance
- Better Water Management
- Integrated Pest Control
- Companion Planting
- Simple and Cost-Effective

In order to build an herb spiral garden of your own, you need first to construct a spiral foundation around which the plants will grow. This is basically just establishing a template that will coerce the plants into growing into the desired spiral design. An easy way to do this is to take rocks, bricks, pieces of wood, or even pieces of cardboard and arrange them in a spiral. You will then plant your crops along the spiral structure already created.

The 4 Steps to Create Your Own Herb Spiral

Materials You Will Need:

Cardboard, Stakes, String, Organic Matter, Compost, Rock Minerals, Seeds, Bricks

1. *Measure/Determine the Spiral's Perimeter*

First, you will need to put your stake into the ground in the general area where you would like to construct your spiral. Select a spot that will have enough room for your spiral arms.

With your stake in place, tie your string around it, and stretch it out to mark the perimeter of your spiral. Next, put another stake in the ground at the endpoint of your string, and tie your string around it. This marks the overall perimeter of your spiral.

2. *Build Your Foundation*

Every structure needs a good foundation—and so does your spiral. So naturally, once your perimeter has been determined, you will want to work on your base. The foundation of any garden is the soil itself. To get that soil into proper shape and, most importantly—eliminate weeds—put your cardboard down around inside the perimeter of your spiral. Soak the cardboard in water to better stick to the ground, speed up decomposition and add valuable carbon to the dirt.

3. *Create the Framework of Your Spiral*

To create your wall structure/framework, you are going to want to start at the very edge of your perimeter. Put down a line of bricks right at the border of the circumference and continue to deposit your rocks/bricks as you make your way to the center in a spiral pattern. Once the basic design has been established, you can then add another layer of bricks on top, if preferable, for a higher wall structure.

4. *Add Soil/Organic Matter and Plants*

Finally, now that everything else is in place, you can add organic material inside the spiral arms, such as mulch or compost, before actually planting your herbs themselves.

Another good idea is to sprinkle some rock minerals on top to help build up the soil.

In addition to the four main steps mentioned above, you could also choose to add a mini pond to your herb spiral. This mini pond is aesthetically pleasing to the eye—but serves many practical purposes as well. For the mini pond will facilitate additional access to water for herbs that may need just a little more H2O than others. A mini pond can be added to the beginning of your herb spiral so that this precious source of water can be used by more thirsty plants situated at the bottom of your spiral. The pond is also great for luring in beneficial bugs—thirsty little critters that could be of great service to the overall health of your garden. You can further this little ecosystem by situating some stately flower-type plants nearby to give the pond a little shade. This is the perfect environment, for example, for many types of caterpillars. They might call your herb spiral garden home and eventually fill it up with a whole bunch of pretty butterflies!

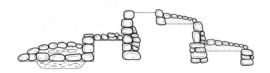

List of potential herbs to plant in your herb spiral:

1. Basil

Most are probably quite familiar with this herb as it's pretty common in kitchen pantries for seasoning. Along with the great taste this herb provides to recipes, it also has amazing antibacterial properties, making it a healthy addition to any garden. This herb loves the sun, so be sure to plant them about mid-spiral so that they can take advantage of direct sunlight.

2. Chives

Chives are another classic herb that makes a great addition to any spiral garden. This herb enjoys the sun just as much as basil, but it's a little hardier as it pertains to shade and does not necessarily have to be in direct sunlight all the time. It's typically best to position them mid-spiral, aiming for either the western or eastern edge of the spiral.

3. Cilantro

Cilantro's a great addition to recipes and also perfect to plant right in the middle of your spiral garden. This herb likes to be greeted by warm sun in the morning but would like a little shade toward the evening. For this reason, the "middle rung" of your spiral would work the best for this particular herb.

4. Dill

Dill has the same temperament as cilantro, seeking sunshine in the dawn's early light while preferring to cool down toward dusk. Another thing to keep in mind is that this herb tends to have a little height to it—so it would be best to plant it further out in the spiral where it will not block sunshine from other plants.

5. Lemon Grass

This herb is a great addition, which seeks out sunshine, but does not need a whole lot of water. This plant typically does well higher up in the spiral, where it can soak up plenty of sun.

6. Mint

Mint should be planted at the low end of the spiral. Mint grows well but needs a good amount of water in order to thrive.

7. Oregano

Unlike mint, oregano tends to thrive in a dry but sunny microclimate. That means it should be placed higher up on the spiral. Being higher up on the spiral arms of the garden allows oregano to drain out excess water while still soaking up a lot of sunshine.

8. Parsley

Parsley is sensitive to the sun and does better when planted on a section of the spiral that gives it adequate shade. Parsley could be planted, for example, next to cilantro since the latter tends to grow tall and provide shade to other nearby plants.

9. Rosemary

Rosemary, similar to oregano, tends to like drier, sunnier microclimates. Having that said, it should also be planted higher up on the spiral so that it can sufficiently drain while still having access to plenty of direct sunlight.

10. Sage

This herb is hardy in a wide variety of environments. It's known, however, to be a great companion plant for oregano, so it would be a great idea to make sage and oregano good neighbors to each other.

11. Tarragon

Tarragon is another herb that needs sun but not a whole lot of water. As such, it should be planted higher up in the spiral garden.

12. Thyme

Thyme's a great companion plant for rosemary. It also likes shade, so it could be placed near a high-growing plant such as cilantro as well.

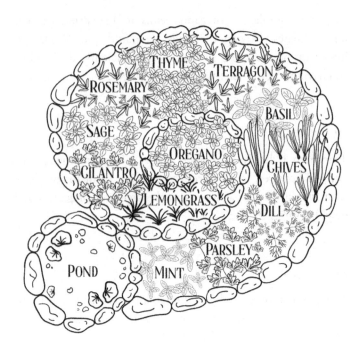

3. *Keyhole Bed*

The "keyhole bed" design is perfect for those looking to save on space. It involves literally structuring your garden in the shape of a "keyhole." This layered structure makes sure to utilize every inch of space, most especially the edges of the keyhole design. In creating this garden bed, it's essential to consider how optimal your planned garden site is. Will there be enough variation in sunshine and shade? Will there be easy access? After these thoughts have been entertained, you should consider the creation of the walls/framework of the structure itself. As is the case with spiral gardens, just about any solid material can be utilized, but rocks and bricks tend to work best.

Next, consider the "core" of your keyhole; this is the cylindri-cal-shaped center that will serve as your "compost bin." Here you can put all manner of beneficial organic material as the nucleus of your soil's health. Around the center will be your "inner layer." This is the section in which your crops will be planted. It's crucial to pay special attention to the "nutrient layers" of the inner layer. The very first covering of this section should be with debris such as sticks, twigs, and other roughage; on top of this can be placed your soil, along with a mixture of fertilizer and other valuable organic material.

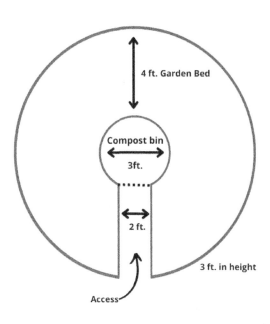

These Plants Will Provide Heaps of Food in a Florida Keyhole Bed:

-Artichokes

-Bamboo

-Basil

-Beans

-Beets

-Berries

-Cabbage

-Carrots

-Coriander

-Chives

-Currents

-Eggplant

-Fennel

-Green beans

-Hibiscus

-Hops

-Horseradish

-Jerusalem artichoke

-Kale

-Lavender

-Marigolds

-Melons

-Mint

-Onions

-Oregano

-Parsley

-Peanuts

-Peppers

-Potatoes

-Raspberry

-Rosemary

-Sage

-Serviceberry

-Strawberry

-Swiss chard

-Sunflowers

-Tomatillo

-Tomato

-Thyme

4. *Hugelkultur*

Hugelkultur is a raised garden bed method that uses a fantastic way to boost garden bed growth—by burying decomposing leaves, wood, and other materials right under the bed. Old decomposing wood from trees provides great nourishment to the soil and is a great way to start out your garden. As odd as it might seem to bury wood under your garden bed, keep in mind that this is simply recreating what takes place in nature. In a forest, dead pieces of leaves and wood come off of trees, fall to the ground, and eventually get covered in a layer of topsoil. Plants then take root and grow on top. It's a quite natural process—with Hugelkultur; we are just giving it a jump start. By planting this kind of roughage under your garden bed, you are providing crucial nutrients to the soil, helping to aerate it, and helping prevent soil erosion. Keep in mind that natural wood is best when it comes to this particular purpose. Treated pieces of timber and cedarwood are not great candidates since they will not break down as quickly as other types. Also, wood from black walnut trees is not advisable either since this type of wood can be toxic to certain plants. Rotten lumber that is already rapidly decomposing would be the best candidate for Hugelkultur. If, for example, you've got an old rotten stump in your backyard. You could take an electric saw, cut the stump pieces out, and then bury them under your garden bed. Just be sure to wear protective glasses because pieces of rotten wood (and any critters that might be lurking inside of it) flying up into your eyes is certainly not fun!

Another thing to consider as it pertains to Hugelkultur is a little something called "sheet mulching." The practice of sheet mulching is in reference to a layered method of applying mulch on a garden bed in which layers of biodegradable organics (such as leaves, wood chips, straw, and the like) are placed on the ground over sheets of newspaper or cardboard. Some have likened these layers of mulch as resembling a batch of "mulch lasagna." You certainly wouldn't want to eat it—but it does make for one heck of a mulch. Furthermore, as the biodegradables decay and decompose, they leave behind several layers of more fertile soil. So even as you bury wood under a garden bed, you can still sheet mulch right on top of it, therefore creating an extremely rich and fertile environment in a relatively short period of time.

Tip: Make your Hugelkultur raised bed 2 or 3 feet tall so the sand underneath won't run off during the rainy season.

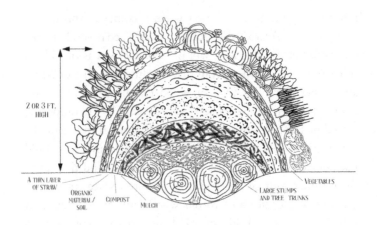

Here are some excellent examples of the types of wood that work best for Hugelkultur:

Alder (Good for All of Florida)
Apple (Good for Northern Florida)
Aspen (Good for All of Florida)
Birch (Good for All of Florida)
Cottonwood (Good for North Florida)
Red Maple and Florida Maple
(Good for Northern and Central Florida)
Poplar (Good for Northern Florida - make sure it's dead so it won't sprout!)

* * *

MAKING USE OF HEDGEROWS IN YOUR GARDEN

The term "hedgerow," just as the name implies, involves growing a straight row of hedge-type shrubs. This is often done on personal properties for aesthetics, as well as for privacy. Instead of building a wooden fence, many opt for growing a perfectly lined up row of hedges. However, hedgerows serve other benefits for permaculture gardening, such as aiding the flow of water and providing protection from wind. They aid in the prevention of soil erosion and create biodiversity by attracting a whole host of beneficial pests.

Hedgerows essentially create their very own microclimates. When used in conjunction with gardening, hedgerows are typically placed right along the edges of the crops as a supportive structure. And you don't necessarily have just to plant a bunch of uniform bushes and shrubs. You could always mix it up into what's been termed a "multifunctional hedgerow."

This method uses a variety of shrubs and trees, as well as several other types of ground-level plants. However, it must be kept in mind that hedgerows require some maintenance. They will need to be trimmed and generally looked after over the long term. This continued trimming makes this "living fence" of edible hedgerows so aesthetically pleasing to look at.

4 excellent types of hedgerow plants for your edible garden:

1. Blueberry
2. Crabapple
3. Elderberry
4. Blackberry

* * *

IN CONSIDERATION OF TRELLIS SUPPORT

The term "trellis" is in reference to any supporting structure that can be made to help facilitate the growth of plants. Such features are especially crucial for climbing plants such as beans and tomatoes, which need something to wrap around as they climb and grow. You can have specially placed tripods, a backyard fence—or heck—even the back of your house could indeed provide trellis-type support for your eagerly growing climbing crops.

As you might have already guessed—in nature, the typical structure for such climbing plants is a tree, shrub, bush, or some other sturdy type of standing plant. It's in the absence of this, that one might want to create their own variation of trellis support. In consideration of construction that might be appropriate, keep in mind that there are three main types of climbers—twining, tendrils, and scrambling.

Twining plants tend to wrap their stems into tight curls and do well with thin support structures. They do not do so well, however, around thicker frames. In the meantime, tendrils are a very interesting type of climber because they use their tendril-like growths to grab hold of nearby structures. These guys can grab hold of stuff and simply hang on for dear life as they spread up and around their supportive trellis.

On the other hand, Scrambling climbers are sturdy vines that scramble out in all directions. These vines can be heavy, and as such, they need a thick and sturdy support structure to hold them up.

Hops and pole beans are good examples of twining plants, whereas grapes, melons, and passion fruit are examples of tendril-type plants. Tomatoes, watermelon, and sweet potatoes, however, constitute the scrambling variety. After you understand the type of climbers you may have, you should plan the design of your trellis accordingly.

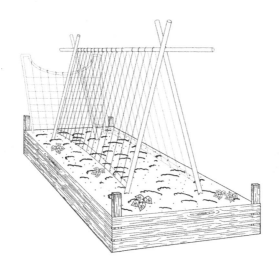

Here are a few ideas:

- *Wall Trellis*

If you've got some climbers that would like to climb right up a wall—then by all means—build them a wall trellis! This sort of design usually entails the creation of an upright, rectangle-shaped framework. Just think of a giant picture frame, and you get the idea.

- *Tent Trellis*

The tent trellis is a framework that takes two entirely equal support structures and places them in a triangular "tent-shaped" arrangement. Heavier, scrambling vine-type plants do well with the tent trellis since they can grow right up the side, then on over the top of the tent-shaped structure.

- *Tipi Trellis*

The Tipi Trellis is really just a classic tripod that allows climbers with heavy hanging fruit such as tomatoes and beans to climb up and around them. These types of climbers really benefit from this kind of support.

* * *

As for the material that should be used for the trellis frameworks, standard wood typically works best. But metal and bamboo could be utilized as well. Be careful with bamboo, however, because it could be prone to excessive rot under certain environmental conditions. So keep this and all of the other tips mentioned in this chapter in mind, as you set about turning your suburban backyard into a winner!

SOME DELICIOUS DECISIONS TO BE MADE...

Decisions... Decisions... Decisions.... Life is chock full of them! And as it pertains to Florida permaculture, the most important decisions you make will undoubtedly be related to its weather and local environment. You might ask yourself—what plants might grow the best in Florida's humid subtropical conditions? How many layers should make up a food forest? And when should you plant them?

You might also wonder just how long your crops need to grow and what kind of soil and nutrients they might need to succeed. Well—wonder no further! Let's go ahead and answer these questions, so you can make the most educated decisions about how to arrange your garden.

Understand Florida's Three Main Growing Seasons

If you live in the sunshine state, you may think that Florida is mostly all about a hot, humid summer and an exceedingly mild winter. But it's actually a little more complicated and nuanced than that. Although it might not seem like it at times —Florida does indeed have the three main seasons of Spring, Summer, and Winter. Furthermore, these seasons vary as you move up the length of the state.

The seasons experienced in the northern panhandle, for example, are much different than what one would experience at the southern tip of Florida near Miami. And just like Florida has three seasons, it also has three growing regions. There is the north, like that aforementioned Florida panhandle, the central region, and Florida's southernmost extremity.

Let's take a closer look at each of them:

North Florida

In the northernmost section of Florida, Spring is the best season to deposit your more tender/sensitive crops into the soil. Hardier, less temperature-sensitive crops, however, can be planted during the winter.

Central Florida

As one might very well imagine, Central Florida often moderates between the two poles of the northern and southern climates. But generally speaking, Spring is a great time to consider planting.

South Florida

As it pertains to south Florida, most crops should be planted in late winter or early Spring. On the other hand, fruit trees can indeed be successfully planted throughout the year, but Spring is the ideal time to do so.

With this in consideration, let's take a look at the seasons:

Spring

The spring season typically runs from January until May. During this time, growers can get one final harvest from hardy winter crops such as leafy greens and other overwintering vegetables before depositing some spring-friendly crops down into the soil. The tricky thing about Florida's spring season is the variation of its "last frost," which could occur sometime in January or sometime in mid-April. As you might imagine, it's up north, in the panhandle region, that typically has a later last frost, while central and southern Florida experiences their last frost typically no later than the middle of March.

Summer

Florida's hot, humid summers are the prime time to grow many classic Florida staples. This season is known for its heat as well as excessive rain. The summer is when many of those fruiting plants will begin to be ready to harvest. However, one must take care to make sure that the crops do not suffer from the summer season's extreme heat. Plenty of morning sun coupled with some afternoon shade is tremendously helpful. Crops should also have plenty of water so that they don't get too dry. Considering these challenges, container crops are sometimes the best option. Container crops, after all, can be more easily moved and modified to withstand harsh heat or dry spells better. A key sign that a plant needs to be given a break from the sun is if they start to droop or fall over. This is an indication of a plant under duress, and they should be provided with some shade as soon as possible. The summer season typically stretches from May to September but varies a bit depending on the region. Northern Florida can have a summer season that doesn't really start until June. Southern Florida, on the other hand, could enter into the summer season as early as April. And Central Florida is perhaps the most persnickety of all since, at times, summer seems to begin in the middle of May only to abruptly halt in October.

Winter

On average, it can be said that Florida's winter season runs from September to March. At this time, one should consider planting some of the hardier variety of leafy greens and herbaceous-type plants. Seedlings for these crops should be planted sometime in late summer. Since Florida's winters can be a little dry, it's important to make sure that these crops are periodically watered. Also, since the sunlight decreases, make sure that these plants are fully exposed to the sun. There's no need for shade during the winter season. Pest management is also a lot easier since bugs significantly decrease during the winter.

* * *

Let the deliciousness begin!

Berries!

I have a soft spot for all kinds of berries. High in fibers loaded with antioxidants, and help fight inflammation...Sounds good, right? Good thing they taste even better!

- Blueberries

Blueberries typically do well in the Florida climate. This sweet treat not only tastes good but is good for you. It has nutrients that are good for your heart and antioxidants that are good for your mind. In addition, studies show that blueberries can be beneficial for memory and other cognitive abilities. But don't forget to plant them in the Spring! Springtime is the best time of year to plant your blueberries in Florida. The blueberries will then ripen and be ready to harvest in June.

- Surinam Cherries

Sometimes also known as the "Brazilian cherry," this crop can grow a whopping 25 feet tall under the warm glow of the Florida sunshine! This plant is best in tropical/subtropical environments, so it would be best suited for primarily South and Central Florida regions. It's possible to grow them further north, but they could very well die if the temperature drops below freezing.

- Mulberries

Mulberries are great crops to plant and typically do well throughout the state of Florida. Mulberries are a crop that actually makes good use of sandy Florida soil, and they can do well even during a particularly dry season. They also do well, whether in bright sunlight or a shadier environment. One of the great things about this plant is the sheer volume of berries that this crop provides. However, keep in mind that this is a slowly developing plant, and if you start out from a seed, it could actually take years before your mulberry begins bearing fruit.

For this reason, many make use of an already grown mulberry and simply add the grafted plant into their garden. Mulberries are also great for food forests because they can produce a ton of valuable mulch. Mulberries can reach up to tree-like stature, or you can regularly trim them and keep them around as a shrub.

- Huckleberries

A close relative of the blueberry—huckleberries can typically be grown without any problem all throughout the state of Florida. The best time to plant them is in the Spring. Huckleberries are known for their deliciously sweet flavor. It's been said that you know when a huckleberry is ripe by how shiny or dull the sheen of the berry is. Ripe berries will look a bit dull in appearance. If they are really shiny, however, this could be an indication that they are not yet ready to be picked.

- Haws

Unofficially known as "Florida's cranberry"—haws do pretty well in Florida's northern panhandle region.

- Gooseberries

Gooseberries require a mild climate and generally do well in Florida. This is a low-maintenance crop, but some minimal trimming/pruning might be occasionally necessary. These berries are known to make a rather delicious jam.

*** * * ***

How to Implement "Food (Forest) Layers" with Your Crops

What is a food forest? The food forest is a crucial aspect of permaculture gardening. From the tops of its trees, way down to the roots below—the food forest provides multiple layers of food for those who grow it on a year-round basis. If you would like to grow a food forest, then you need to be acquainted with the many idiosyncrasies that are involved in its establishment as well as its maintenance. So let's take a more in-depth look at how the layers of a food forest function.

Starting from the top:

Tall Tree Layer

The tall tree layer of your food forest is the top layer. This is the literal canopy of your food forest garden. These trees are best served planted on the northern edge of your garden. Every lower layer of your food forest should then be planted just south of the tall tree layer.

- Avocado Tree - *Persea Americana*

The avocado excels in Central and South Florida. It's not widely known, but the avocado is one of Florida's top agricultural products right behind oranges. The types of avocados that grow well in Florida are the following varieties: Donnie, Dupuis, Hardee, Pollock, Simmonds, Russell, Lula, Choquette, and Monroe. The avocado itself is actually a large berry, with a large, rock-solid seed in the center, while the rest of the fruit's innards is comprised of a light green "creamy pulp." It's that green, creamy pulp that folks find so tasty in dishes such as "guacamole." As it pertains to the Avocado Tree that the avocado comes from, it does quite well in Florida's sandier soils.

It's important to make sure you do not plant the trees in a section of land prone to frequent flooding. These trees need to be planted in a spot with proper drainage. The trees should also be positioned to receive direct sunlight and given adequate space away from any other nearby trees. These trees are perennial, and the best time to plant them is in the early spring season. Harvest time arrives around August at the height of the summer when the avocados are dark green in color.

- Tamarind Tree - *Tamarindus indica*

Grown in South Florida, the Tamarind Tree is a robust perennial to place as the top layer of your food forest. The best time to plant this tree is during the spring and summer seasons. And did you know Tamarind can help prevent osteoporosis? This is because it's filled with vitamins and minerals such as magnesium, vitamin D, and calcium.

- Pecan Tree - *Carya illinoinensis*

Pecan trees excel in North and Central Florida. Along with providing pecans, they also offer a great source of shade and protection for other underlying crops. These trees are perennial, and the best time to plant them is in early Spring. The two best varieties that can be grown are the "Elliott" and "Amling" pecan trees. Eliot trees are great, but you must ensure they are positioned higher than the local water table, so the roots aren't flooded. These trees are considered "drought-tolerant" and have a great degree of "wind resistance."

Along with all of this, the tasty nuts that Eliot trees produce are also quite desirable. The Amling pecan tree, on the other hand, is a great "pollinator tree" to pair the Elliot pecan tree with. The trees don't have to be planted close in order to cross-pollinate. In fact, they can be planted as far as a mile apart, and pollen borne aloft on the wind will still do the trick.

- Loquat Tree - *Eriobotrya japonica*

The Loquat Tree is an excellent choice for the top layer of your food garden and can grow quite well throughout Florida. This tree is a perennial, and the best time to plant it is from mid to late Spring. Loquat trees are fairly low maintenance, are aesthetically pleasing, and produce tasty fruit. For the Loquat, it's best not to start off from the seedling because growth from the seed can be rather slow. It's better to make use of a grafted plant instead. Some of the best types to plant are: Wolfe, Thursby, Tanaka, Oliver, Judith, Emanuel, Golden Nugget, Goliath, and Champagne.

- Mulberry Tree - *Morus alba*

The Mulberry Tree is yet another perennial that can be grown statewide in Florida. The best time to plant is during the Spring season. Good varieties to choose from are: Tice, Pakistan, Tehama, King White Pakistan, Shangri-Law, Bachuus Noir, Red Gelato, and Black Persian. Beware that this tree can reach up to 80ft!

- Pawpaw Tree - *Asimina triloba*

This American native fruit also grows well throughout the sunshine state, and it too is a perennial. The pawpaw should be planted in the Spring. Varieties suitable for Florida growth are: small flower pawpaw, dwarf pawpaw, wooly pawpaw, slim leaf pawpaw, netted pawpaw, four-petaled pawpaw, and last but not least—common pawpaw. Also known as "Poor man's banana," this nutritional fruit is packed with magnesium, iron, vitamin C, manganese, and copper.

- Papaya Tree - *Carica papaya*

The papaya tree can be grown in either Central or South Florida, but northern Florida is just a bit too cold. If it gets at or below freezing, these trees might die. So yes, it's best to keep them in the warmer climates of the state. Papaya is a perennial plant and needs to be planted by the time Spring comes around. If more than one tree is planted, make sure they are situated about 10 feet apart. Also, be sure to grow them in direct sunlight. Care must also be taken to ensure that they are not planted in a region prone to flooding. Some pest control for these trees might be necessary since the so-called "papaya fruit fly" can, at times, become quite a nuisance. The fly lays its eggs in fruit, and once they hatch, they devour the papayas. A papaya tree full of rotten fruit isn't exactly a pretty sight, so you really want to quickly address a fruit fly infestation as soon as possible. The simplest means of controling these pests is to prevent access to the fruit they crave. This involves wrapping fruit in paper bags. It might look a little strange to have paper bags hanging off your trees, but if it keeps these pests at bay—it's well worth the effort. At any rate, it may take several months before you can harvest fruit from your papaya trees. The main papaya tree varieties are: maradol, red lady, and tainung #2.

- Peach Tree - *Prunus persica*

Peach trees work great in North and Central Florida. Peaches start to run into trouble, however, if you try to grow them in South Florida, and is therefore not recommended. Peach trees need to be positioned in direct sunlight and away from flood-prone terrain. Having that said, a peach tree planted downhill from a slope probably wouldn't be a good idea since the rain would invariably send water flooding down to the tree. Peach trees are perennial and should be planted in either early winter or early Spring. Be sure to prune your peach trees regularly to prevent overgrowth. Varieties include: Florida prince, Florida crest, sunblest, UF gold, and UF sun.

- Mamey Sapote Tree - *Pouteria sapota*

These trees can be grown in South Florida and are perennials. They should be planted in the springtime. Here are the best varieties to work with: Pantin, Pace, Viejo, and Magana. Some say it resembles the flavor of sweet potato with a hint of peach and apricot. This South American beauty can grow up to 40ft in Florida.

Low (Smaller) Tree Layer

The low tree layer is the repository of smaller trees, such as smaller fruit-bearing trees, berry and cherry-bearing shrubs, and dwarf fruit trees. Besides bearing fruit, these trees can serve the purpose of shoring up the strength of the soil and enriching it with nitrogen. They can also serve as pollinators and ward off intrusive pests.

- Moringa Tree (Also known as Horseradish tree and 'Tree of Life') - *Moringa oleifera*

This tree grows all throughout Florida and is a perennial. The best time to plant it—is in mid to late Spring. One of the more exciting things about this crop is its sheer nutritional value. Just one fruit from this tree is loaded with Vitamin C, Vitamin A, Potassium, protein, and even a hearty helping of calcium. It seems that this fruit has just about everything you need for a healthy life. Well, I guess it's no wonder then that they've dubbed the Moringa—the Tree of Life! Even so, there is an element of this tree that could bring death. Because in all seriousness, be advised that the root of this tree can be toxic. So yes, whatever you do, don't eat the root of the Moringa Tree.

- Banana Tree - *Musa*

The Banana tree grows throughout the sunshine state and is perennial. Even though we call this crop a "tree," it's important to note that it's actually an herb with a large "trunk-like pseu-dostem" which consists of a series of interwoven leaves that closely intersect with each other. The flowering stalks on top bear the bananas we all know and love. Since this crop has its origin in the rainforest, it loves sunshine and humidity. The best time to plant this crop is in the Spring or summer. The best varieties are: Dwarf Cavendish, Mahoi, north and central Namwa, Pisang Raja, Raga Puri, Ice Cream, and Gold Finger.

- Sugar Apple Tree - *Annona squamosa*

A native of the tropics—the best bet for Sugar apple trees is South Florida. But there are some regions of Central Florida where they could grow as well. This tree is perennial and needs to be planted in Spring. The tree should not be planted in a flood-prone area, as excessive moisture could cause rot and even kill the plant. The tree can survive for long stretches without water, but a prolonged lack of moisture will ultimately stunt its growth and cause it to drop its leaves, preventing fruit from properly form-ing. Normally, the fruit from this tree comes in a variety of shapes. Some are round, and some are ovate. Others are conical, and still, more are heart-shaped. The fruit is truly delicious, with a very sweet flavor no matter how they are shaped. Varieties of sugar apple trees are: Thai Lessard and Kampong Mauve.

- Fig Tree - *Ficus carica*

Fig trees are best grown in South Florida. Not native to the Americas, the figs were introduced by Europeans in the 16th Century. This sun-loving crop is perennial and can be planted anytime between late winter and early Spring. The type grown in Florida is typically a kind of "multi-branched" shrub. Fig trees like to spread out and provide plenty of shade, so surrounding plants in the food garden should be situated according to their needs. Some notable varieties of fig trees are: San Pedro, Smyrna, and Caprifigs.

- Barbados Cherry Tree - *Malpighia emarginata*

Barbados cherry trees are best grown in South Florida. They are perennial and work best if planted during the Spring. I love to get myself a handful of these and just munch them while making dinner. The only downside is that the pit takes up half of the fruit!

- Mango Tree - *Mangifera*

Mango trees are perennial and do well in both South and Central Florida. They can be planted anytime from early Spring to well into the summer season. Some of the best (and sweetest) mango varieties are: Carabao, Haden, Kent, Keitt, and Tommy Atkins. I must say that mangos also have a special place in my heart... it's my favorite fruit! Once you get your hands on your first harvest of Carabao, you'll never want to buy supermarket mangos ever again.

- Indian Curry Tree - *Murraya koenigii*

Indian curry trees are perennial and grow well in South Florida. It's best to plant them over the winter season. Instead of using store-bought curry powder, sprinkle 8 to 10 of these leaves in your curry, and you'll have a fragrant, antioxidant-packed meal ready to go!

- Persimmons Tree - *Diospyros virginiana*

The persimmon tree grows well throughout Florida and is perennial. It should be planted between late winter and early Spring. Just be sure not to pick the fruit from this tree too soon. They taste best once they get soft and really ripe. This typically occurs right before the fruit is about to drop from the tree. Some notable varieties include: Fuyu and Asian Persimmon. Black sapote is also a great choice (and my favorite!). Its delicious taste resembles the flavor of chocolate pudding, hence why some people call it "chocolate pudding fruit." You really can't beat a flavor like that for something that quite literally grows on trees!

Shrub Layer

Immediately below the low tree layer of your food forest, you find your shrub layer. Shrubs are another valuable part of the food forest ecosystem, aiding the soil through rich infusions of nitrogen. Plenty of good fruit-bearing shrubs and bushes can be found in this layer. Here are some examples:

- Lots and Lots of Berries!

As mentioned earlier in this book, berries can play a vital role in your garden. And blueberries, mulberries, huckleberries, and gooseberries; to name a few—are all great additions to a shrub layer in a food forest. But you also might want to include: beautyberry, seagrape, hibiscus, pennyroyal, wild berries, and even wild coffee!

- Cassava plant - *Manihot esculenta*

Cassava plant (also known as Yuca) is perennial and grows throughout all of Florida. In addition to being in the shrub layer, it is also an excellent groundcover. It will take around 6 to 7 months to harvest.

What I love most about this plant is the fact that it is tolerant to drought and grows beautifully in poor soil.

- Katuk plant - *Sauropus androgynus*

The Katuk plant is a perennial that generally does well in both South and Central Florida. It should be planted during the Spring. Katuk is incredibly nutritious, especially for nursing mothers, as it can stimulate milk production.

- Chaya plant - *Cnidoscolus aconitifolius*

Chaya is another perennial which is good in South and Central Florida. This plant is also an early starter, so be sure to plant it as soon as springtime arrives. Maple leaf and Deep lobe are both great varieties of this crop.

- Prickly pears - *Opuntia wentiana*

Perennial prickly pears thrive in South Florida. They can be planted in both Spring and summer. The best varieties for Florida are: Indian Fig, Purple Prickly Pear, Naranjona, and Yellow Platanera. They are ready to be harvested in Summer.

When I was young, my dad used to bring home pounds and pounds of this spiky fruit. I was his little helper, and my job was to get the fruit out of the "shell" while he would hold the thorny exterior. Barehanded.

- Broccoli - *Brassica oleracea var. italica*

Broccoli is an annual crop that grows well in Central and Northern Florida. This crop is best suited if first planted over the winter season. Florida varieties are: De Cicco, Calabrese, Early Green, Early Dividend, Packman, and Waltham 29. It will take 2 to 3 months to harvest.

Did you know that the Italians introduced this crop to America? Pizza, pasta, and broccoli! Yum!

- Eggplant - *Solanum melongena*

The eggplant is perennial and grows well in both South and Central Florida. This crop should be planted in the spring season. Varieties that grow well in Florida are: Dusky, Ichiban, Black Beauty, Bambino (dwarf), Astrakom, and Casper.

This berry (yes, eggplants are considered fruits) can grow over 2 years.

- Key Lime Tree - *Citrus* × *aurantifolia*

This perennial crop works well in South Florida and should be planted anytime from early Spring to the Summer season. Ready to make a key lime pie?

- Squash - *Cucurbita*

Squash grows primarily in Central and North Florida but can also manage to overwinter in South Florida if necessary. Florida-grown varieties of squash include: Chayote, Crookneck, and Waltham. It can be harvested 45 to 60 days after planting. It is also related to the melon family.

- Cranberry Hibiscus - *Hibiscus acetosella*

Cranberry hibiscus is perennial and can grow all throughout the state of Florida. It should be planted by late Spring. You can eat the leaves cooked or raw. Or simply brew tea.

- Tea!

Tea plants can be successfully grown in any region of Florida. They should be planted during the Spring season. Some common varieties include: Chamomile, Jasmine, and Lemon Balm.

Herbaceous Layer

The herbaceous layer of a food garden is made up of "low growing" herbs and other plants. These crops are good for the soil as they provide ready-made "living mulch" as they shed their organic debris. They also provide nitrogen to the earth and aid in the retention of moisture. These herbs can also play a role in both the attraction of pollinating insects as well as the prevention of harmful pests. Here are some examples:

- Kale - *Brassica oleracea*

Kale is biennial and thrives in North and Central Florida. It should be planted by early Spring. A few varieties are: Tuscan, Red Russian, and Winterbor. This superfood can be harvested in approximately 60 days.

- Swiss Chard - *Beta vulgaris convar. cicla*

Swiss chard is biennial and can be found throughout Florida. This crop is best when planted in the spring season. Florida varieties include: Italian Withe Ribbed, Bright Lights, Erbette, and Fordhook Giant. 2 to 3 months to harvest.

Toss the leaves in a salad or eat them cooked.

- Brussel Sprouts - *Brassica oleracea var. gemmifera*

Brussel Sprouts are biennial and grow well in North Florida. The best season to plant them in mid to late summer. Jade Cross and Long Island are two varieties that grow pretty well in Florida, and they will need three months to be harvested.

- Beans - *Phaseolus vulgaris*

Beans are an annual plant that can be grown throughout the state of Florida. Since beans are naturally loaded with nitrogen, they are great additions to any garden's soil. Keep in mind that these beans need a lot of sun and plenty of water. They don't need to be flooded though, so make sure the soil can drain itself appropriately. A few varieties are: Bush Blue Lake, Roma II, Contender, Pinto Beans, Lima Beans, and Cherokee Wax. Beans can also belong in the groundcover layer (Southern peas) and in the vertical layer – Florida-friendly pole bean varieties: McCaslan, Kentucky Wonder, and Blue Lake.

- Peas - *Pisum sativum*

Peas are annual and generally do well in South and Central Florida. It's best to plant them in the Spring season. It'll take 60 to 70 days to harvest them, just like beans.

- Collards - *Brassica oleracea var. Viridis*

Collards grow well in Central Florida. The best time to plant them is in early Spring. Georgia Southern and the Yates Strain, are varieties that generally grow well in Florida.

My favorite dish to this day is my mom's open-fire cabbage soup.

From the garden straight to the pot.

- Herbs!

These flavorsome perennials are best to start between Fall and late Spring.

The ones that exceed in Florida are: Basil, Cilantro, Dill, Lemon Balm, Mint, Oregano, Parsley, Rosemary, Tarragon, and Thyme.

- Lemongrass - *Cymbopogon*

This perennial plant is not only nutritious, but it's also a mosquito repeller! It can be grown all throughout Florida, and it's advisable to start it in the Spring. This one not only is a nasty bug repeller but at the same time attracts honeybees! Lemongrass is a must-have in your garden.

- Peppers - *Capsicum*

Peppers are on the herbaceous layer but are also considered a fantastic groundcover.

Early Spring is the best time to plant these annuals. Florida-friendly sweet pepper varieties include: California wonder, Red Knight, Big Bertha, Sweet Banana, Giant Marconi, and Cubanelle. On the polar opposite, you can find great hot pepper varieties like: Early Jalapeno, Cherry Bomb, Hungarian Hot Wax, Big Chile II, Mariachi, Numex, Ancho, Thai, Anaheim Chile, Long Cayenne, Habanero, and Caribbean Red Habanero.

Sweet peppers can take 2 to 3 months to be ready to harvest but hot peppers will take longer—around 5 months.

Groundcover layer

The groundcover layer is also made of low-growing plants, but these plants spread more horizontally to—like the name implies—better cover the ground. Some examples of these low-lying plants include:

- Tomato - *Solanum Lycopersicum*

Tomatoes are an annual plant and typically do well in both North and Central Florida. They should be planted in Spring. My favorite ones include: Amelia, Better Boy, Celebrity, and Roma. Heat Wave II grows exceedingly well in the hotter months. It belongs to the groundcover layer and the vertical layer.

- Brazilian Spinach - *Alternanthera sissoo*
- New Zealand spinach - *Tetragonia tetragonioides*
- Okinawa spinach - *Gynura bicolor*

These 3 Florida-friendly types of spinach are perennials that grow well in North and Central Florida. It's best to plant them in late Summer.

- Seminole Pumpkin - *Cucurbita moschata*

This native Floridian is perennial and can be planted throughout the state. It could also work as a part of the food forest's "vertical layer." Any time of the year is good to plant this pumpkin (except in the "frosty" months), and it will be ready to harvest after 90 days.

- Jerusalem Artichoke - *Helianthus tuberosus*

This is a perennial plant that thrives in both North and Central Florida. It does best if planted in Spring. It's an amazing electrolyte and mineral source, and its roots are delicious when roasted.

- Mint - *Mentha*

Mint crops grow throughout Florida. They are perennial and should be planted in the Spring season. Peppermint and Spearmint both grow fairly well in Florida.

Root Layer

The root layer is underneath the ground, where the roots of plants reside. Crops with sturdy, deep roots, such as carrots and turnips, are great for holding in the soil and better aiding in soil retention. Let's take a look at some of these a little more in-depth:

- Garlic - *Allium sativum*

Garlic is perennial and can grow throughout the state of Florida. It's best if garlic is planted during the winter season. Types that do well in Florida: Romanian Red, Creole, Georgian Crystal, and Thermadrone.

- Onions - *Allium cepa*

Onions are another perennial that can be found growing all over the sunshine state. They, too, tend to do well if planted in the winter. Some best varieties are: Excel, Crystal Wax Bermuda, Granex Yellow, and Granex White.

- Turmeric - *Curcuma longa*

Turmeric is a perennial root crop that can be grown throughout Florida. It should be planted in early Spring. This superfood has plenty of medicinal properties. It is a natural anti-inflammatory and antioxidant and even helps prevent cancer and Alzheimer's. All hail Turmeric!

- Ginger - *Zingiber officinale*

Ginger is perennial and grows in every region of Florida. It, too, should be planted during the Spring season. To harvest it, you have to dig out the entire plant (the same as turmeric). Ginger reaches full maturity after 8 or 10 months.

- Turnips - *Brassica rapa ssp. rapa*

Turnips grow all over the state of Florida and are annuals. They should be planted during the winter season. The best kind to plant in Florida is the "Purple Top" variety. The same goes for beetroots (best Florida-friendly varieties: Detroit supreme and Detroit dark red).

- Sweet potato - *Ipomoea batatas*

Types of varieties of sweet potato that grow well in Florida are: Beauregard and Centennial. This perennial thrives all over Florida and can even be eaten raw. The greens are excellent when cooked.

- Carrots - *Daucus carota*

Carrots are annual plants that can grow in both North and Central Florida. They should be planted during the spring season. They need direct sunlight, and the sprouting seeds need a lot of moisture. It may take a couple of weeks for them to sprout. Also, be sure not to plant them too deep! You will want to eventually harvest them after all—not excavate them! Some of the best varieties to grow are: Nantes Half Long, Chantenay Royal, and Imperator 58.

Vertical Layer

The vertical layer of the food garden is made up of climbing plants that reach from the bottom of the food forest all the way up to the top. These crops climb on existing structures and provide their unique benefits along the way.

- Sugar Cane - *Saccharum officinarum*

Sugar Cane is versatile enough to be able to be grown in North, Central, and South Florida. This crop is a perennial that needs to be planted in late summer. Growing up, my father would cut out the peel and simply give us chunks of sugar cane for us to chew on. It's a low-cost (and delicious!) snack. Sugar cane also has the benefit of being a fantastic hedgerow.

- Passion Fruit - *Passiflora edulis*

Passion Fruit is a perennial that grows in South and Central Florida. This crop should be planted in Spring. Some varieties are: Yellow Passion Fruit, Purple Passion Fruit, and Giant Granadilla. You can expect the fruit to ripen in 70 to 80 days after pollination occurs.

- Muscadine Grapes - *Vitis rotundifolia*

This perennial plant grows exceptionally well in Central and North Florida. It's best to plant them during the spring season. These grapes make up a very rich and fragrant wine.

- Yams - *genus Dioscorea*

Yams are perennials that can be grown in Central and South Florida. This starchy tuber is best served when planted during the Spring. They can take 6 months to be harvested, but some types take up to 2 years!

The Role of Animals in Permaculture

The Animal Kingdom plays a vital role in permaculture. And when we speak of the Animal Kingdom here—we're not just talking about squirrels and rabbits—but also bugs. Yes, those fascinating slimy little critters of the creepy-crawly kind. We may not always like being around them, but even bugs play a critical role in sustaining an ecological garden.

In fact, they play a critical role for the whole planet. If all bugs were to perish tomorrow—the world wouldn't last too much longer. For without the intervention of pollinating insects, much of the world's vegetation would be in trouble. So, without any further ado—here in this chapter, we will demonstrate to you just how vital animals and insects are to your garden.

Pollinators—Not Just Your Friendly Honeybee

For the growing of fruit and flowers, the end goal of growing these crops is to have an abundant harvest. And to do so, they must be adequately pollinated. Honeybees naturally come to mind when we consider this pollination. We see these busy tiny insects flitting from plant to plant, spreading all of that pollen goodness (unless you're allergic!) all over the place.

But it's not just honeybees that pollinate our crops. Bigger creatures such as butterflies, hummingbirds, rodents, rabbits, and even deer can serve as pollinators to some degree as well. However, some pollinators can also be pests, so we may not appreciate their presence in our gardens year-round.

As beautiful as the butterfly is, for example, its predecessor in life—the caterpillar—is a notorious garden pest. This hungry critter can take a massive bite out of the leafy greens in your garden. But as much as we are wary of an insect-like this, munching on our veggies, it is indeed a valuable part of the overall ecosystem.

Here are some methods you can use to keep those pollinators coming:

* *Flower Beds a Plenty*

Flowers are natural attractors of pollinators. And flowers can significantly enhance the biodiversity of the kind of pollinators that you attract. Depending on the flowers involved, your beds might attract everything from bumblebees and hoverflies to ladybugs and butterflies. It's the mighty yet humble bumblebee, which will always remain one of the best pollinators on the planet. As you plant your flowers, keep in mind the pollinators they might attract and arrange them accordingly. You might want to grow a flower bed on the edge of your crops to boost their pollination.

- *Make Use of Hedgerows*

Hedgerows are another notable mention because they are perfect for creating their own microclimate/ecosystems right at the edge of your garden, along with attracting pollinators. Hedgerows were designed with the idea of marking boundaries, and have often been used as a so-called "living fence." But as much as they keep some nasty pests out, they also draw beneficial pollinators in. Beneficial insects, rodents, and birds might decide to make themselves at home in your hedgerows.

- *Utilize "Wild" Sections of Your Garden*

Even parts of your garden that are overgrown and perhaps a little wild could serve as a great habitat for pollinators. These pollinators will then make trips back and forth between your garden and the surrounding wilderness. If, for example, you have an overgrown woodsy area at the edge of your backyard —don't worry. The overgrown shrubs, bushes, and grasses back there can host a wide variety of pollinators. These nearby ecosystems are sometimes referred to as "stepping stones" because they are just a stone's throw away from your garden, and it's quite easy for helpful little critters to travel back and forth between the two.

BRING ON THE BENEFICIAL BUG ATTRACTORS!

Bugs and plants have had a symbiotic relationship for millions of years. We don't want to get into a metaphysical debate here, but like just about everything else on this planet, it seems to have been made with a rather specific design in mind.

Pollinators are looking for nectar, pollen, and natural habitat. The plant life they frequent in the meantime is being benefited by the fact that these bugs carry pollen back and forth from plant to plant. Certain plants naturally go hand in hand with certain bugs. So, let's take a look at some of the best beneficial bug-attracting crops that we can plant in Florida.

- Anise Hyssop

Anise Hyssop is a durable plant and can tough it out in the dry season. It grows beautiful foliage that draws both the eyes of admirers and the attention of pollinating insects.

- Black-Eyed Susan

This wild growing flower loves the sun but doesn't need much water. It regularly attracts plenty of pollinating butterflies and bees.

- Cannas

This is a perennial pollinator-attracting plant that loves the Florida sun. Cannas are also quite aesthetically appealing, with vibrant colors that enhance the landscape.

- Coral Honeysuckle

Coral Honeysuckle is a standard staple of Florida. You can see these growing just about anywhere there's a good amount of sunlight. As you might guess, these plants also attract plenty of pollinators that can be seen flying in and out of its iconic honeysuckle flowers.

- Marigolds

Marigolds are beautiful, rather ubiquitous flowers that bloom annually in the great state of Florida. They are also great attractors of beneficial pollinators. Therefore, it's quite helpful to strategically plant batches of marigolds around crops that you would like to benefit from increased pollination. Marigolds are also great as a deterrent since they repel harmful nematodes in the soil.

- Nasturtium

Nasturtiums are another annual plant in Florida. They boast pretty orange, red, and yellow flowers that regularly attract pollinators.

- Passion Flower

Passion Flower is a perennial crop that grows well and sports beautiful flowers suitable for pollinating critters.

- Pentas

Pentas grow perennially and provide colorful flowers that pollinating butterflies absolutely love.

- Mint

This herb is beloved by many pollinators and grows quite well in the parts of Florida with high humidity. Just be careful, for this hardy herb grows fast and can rapidly multiply. Don't let it overpower the rest of your crops.

- Oregano

Oregano is another herb that can attract plenty of pollinating critters. It's not only good for your pasta but also good for pollination!

- Fennel

Fennel is a perennial plant that attracts pollinators and brings a wide variety of other beneficial bugs to the garden. Beetles, wasps, and ants are attracted to the bright yellow fennel flowers. Quite a few birds are also attracted to fennel since they like to feed on all of those tasty fennel seeds.

- Hogweed

Hogweed gets its name because it was commonly used to feed pigs. But as unappealing as "hogweed" might sound, this crop is actually quite beneficial for your garden. And one of the beneficial bugs that it attracts are hoverflies. Hoverflies are pollinators with a dual purpose because, along with spreading pollen, they also serve as predators against other harmful pests.

- Buttonbush

The Buttonbush is actually a shrub. It thrives in somewhat wetter conditions and is an ideal attractor of a wide variety of pollinating insects.

RABBITS AND GOATS—THE ALL-NATURAL WEED EATERS!

Weeds are the bane of any good gardener. And the proposed solutions are often even worse than the problem. Commercial weed killers are a quick fix at best and have long-term consequences at worst. The chemicals go deep into the soil, and even while temporarily putting down weeds, they can throw the ecological balance severely out of whack.

Even worse, you could just be making your weeds even more formidable since, after a while, they develop some immunity to whatever chemical you are dumping, only to grow back stronger than ever. Manually pulling or cutting weeds is perhaps preferable, but such labor is tedious and time-consuming.

Instead of going to all of this trouble, wouldn't it be great if there was some creature out there that would get rid of weeds for you—not as a favor—but simply because it's something that it naturally loves to do? Well, look no further, my friends, because such a creature does indeed exist.

Both rabbits and goats happen to love munching on weeds. And if you've ever seen a rabbit slurping up dandelion stems as if they're spaghetti—it's also quite entertaining to watch. These rabbits hop right over to those yellow eyesores, put their mouth down low to the ground, cut the bottom of the stem with their scissor-like teeth, and then slurp that dandelion up bottom first as if it were fettuccini. It's great.

A word of caution with rabbits, however, you need to make sure they can't get access to your main garden vegetables. Because along with eating weeds, they would gladly eat those too. Preventive measures such as wrapping chicken wire around choice crops would be beneficial so that these bunnies can munch on wild-growing weeds without disturbing the crops you would wish to grow.

Goats are another all-natural option for getting rid of weeds. Goats are prolific eaters and are known to eat just about anything. And they do it quite rapidly! As with the rabbits, make sure you take protective measures for your actual crops because you don't want these hungry mammals eating up your whole garden even while they devour your weeds!

ALL YOU NEED TO KNOW ABOUT VERMICOMPOSTING

Vermicomposting—the name may not sound all that appealing, but it's a great way to shape up your garden! This process makes use of earthworms to create a rich and sustainable environment for your soil. Earworm waste—otherwise known as "castings"—are incredibly rich in nitrogen and other essential nutrients. Vermicomposting seeks to make the best of this precious gardening resource.

. . .

Worms are placed in traditional compost made up of organic debris (like kitchen scraps) and allowed to do their business in peace. The worms digest compost already present and then produce waste that is even more potent compost than it was in its original form. The resulting soil is highly nutritious and loaded with beneficial bacteria.

These castings leave the soil with an overall better-defined structure, which has better aeration and can drain well while still being able to hold adequate amounts of water. In short— Vermicomposting is the perfect way to get rid of what would otherwise be garbage by making it into super-rich fertilizer.

There are two main techniques to separate worms from their castings:

- *The "Pyramid" technique*

This method involves taking a compost bin that has already been successfully transformed into worm castings and then dumping the whole thing out on top of a tarp. The material is then left out in the sun to dry. Now form a pyramid-type heap out of the material on the tarp and watch your worms gravitate toward the pyramid to get away from the light. The worms will automatically burrow deep within the pyramid, allowing you to have easy—worm-free—access to the compost surface. After this occurs, you can then swipe the surface layer of castings off the pyramid's sides to collect as compost. Shortly thereafter, the worms will return to burrowing. Just repeat these steps as much as necessary.

- *The "Let the worms decide" technique*

This technique is just about as simple as it sounds. It involves allowing the worms to go at it independently with very minimal intervention. This is the most "natural" method—since, in natural untamed ecosystems, there typically aren't any big critters called humans directing the act of earthworms and their biodegrading debris on a global scale.

The Top Five Vermicomposting Worms for Florida

- Red wiggler

Also, sometimes called the "tiger worm," this little guy knows how to take a bite out of some compost! They are known to digest it rapidly, and quickly produce worm castings. These worms are also highly reproductive, enabling the gardener to breed more of them easily.

- Indian blue

This worm also digests compost quickly, but they are a little more finicky than some other worms. This means that there is a greater chance that they might decide to jump ship and attempt to leave your pile of compost before the job is finished if something in the environment does not entirely please them.

- Alabama jumper

The Alabama jumper is actually an invasive species that ended up in the state of Florida. This worm is good at making short work of leaves and other leafy debris.

- African nightcrawler

This worm rapidly produces castings, as well as copies of each other. Their high reproductive rate makes them ideal for those wishing to breed more worms. The main drawback of these worms is that they require fairly warm temperatures in order to function. If it drops below 60 degrees in fact, they begin to perish. So they might not work out too well in the panhandle region of northern Florida.

- European nightcrawler

The European nightcrawler is relatively big as far as worms go, and it's quite good at munching through compost. However, these worms are not good breeders and are slower than other worms as it pertains to the creation of castings. They are unaffected by cooler drops in temperature so they might be a go-to choice in North Florida—especially during the winter months.

Animals do indeed play a vital role in the health of any would-be garden. We can try to "take control" and do things "our way," but in the end, we really could use the aid of some helpful little critters from the animal kingdom. Please keep all of these suggestions in mind as you set about crafting a sustainable and ecologically friendly garden of your own.

How to Join a
Permaculture
Community

L ife is all about community and connection. And as it pertains to permaculture, we find that the same sentiment very much holds true. Just as you have worked to create an ecosystem for your garden in which all of the individual pieces work together as a collective whole—you too are part of a larger community. You are not on an ecological island just fending for yourself. There is a whole permaculture community waiting to join you.

Permaculture finds ways to link elements of the environment closer together, and it can also foster close personal connections among enthusiasts. For this reason, any budding permaculturist should always abide by the principle of "integrate rather than segregate."

Don't hide your agricultural triumphs from the world—share them with the community!

And since you can't always expect people to come to you— you might have to figure out ways to go to them. Having that said, here are some ideas of how you could become more involved in your local permaculture community:

- *Socialize at Local Farmers' Markets*

Sometimes the best way to meet other permaculture enthusiasts is simply to get to know people at local farmers' markets. The farmers market brings you around like-minded people who indicate that they have a keen interest in farm-grown crops by their very presence. Their curiosity will vary from mildly interested enough in crops for their own personal consumption to being greatly interested in growing a wide variety of crops on their own. If you are going to find a budding permaculturist anywhere—the farmers' market is a good enough place to try as any.

- *Talk to the Experts at Supply Shops*

Similar to the farmer's market, there are no doubt folks of a similar mind and interest down at your local garden supply store. Here, you will find people purchasing products and chit-chatting about the best techniques and methods to keep their gardens alive and well.

Not everyone here may agree on methodology, but the fact that this very subject matter is being brought up is the perfect opportunity for you to quite literally enter the conversation. Strike up a dialogue with those you encounter at your local supply shops, and you may get a few priceless words of wisdom, as well as forge some lasting connections in your local community.

- *Attend Local Permaculture Events*

Permaculture events provide a great way to get to know others in your communities. These gatherings, sometimes known as "convergences," occur all over the country. You might want to look up more information about the local events scheduled in your own region to see when an event might be taking place near you. An easy way to do so is to simply search through recent events/meetings through a social media platform such as Meetup.com. Just a quick search here, and one is inundated with a vast list of permaculture events both near and far.

- *Do Volunteer Work for the Community*

Another great way to get involved in the community is simply by volunteering for the community. If there are any community agricultural projects in need of volunteers, this could be an excellent opportunity for you to get more directly involved. There are often many local cooperatives that could use an extra hand planting at parks or doing some sort of landscaping.

I can recall back in college, taking a few courses that signed me up for just this sort of operation. As part of our course credit, we volunteered time at a local greenhouse, just helping with the general maintenance of the crops. The work was admittedly a bit tedious, but it was indeed good to be able to rub shoulders with those actively involved in gardening on a large scale.

And I can recall that those running the greenhouse were quite enthused to have some extra helping hands. In many ways, being a volunteer is the best possible way to meet people. It immediately puts you on the right foot with those who run the project since you volunteer your time.

Share with Thy Neighbor - Community Gardens

Yes, share and share-alike. Sounds great, doesn't it? But what exactly is a community garden? As simple as it sounds, a community garden is essentially a shared plot of land where folks from a local neighborhood community can grow and harvest crops and—in some instances—even raise some farm animals.

Community gardens can vary in scope and size considerably. Some might be rather small, while others could be quite expansive. Community gardens in urban areas that are much more limited in space are understandably enough, usually much smaller in size. These smaller-scale community gardens might consist of a tiny plot of land in which several locals have placed row upon row of raised gardens. Some community gardens may even be indoors through the use of specially made greenhouses.

On the other hand, rural communities could potentially have several acres allotted for a community garden project. But no matter how big or small, community gardens do indeed create a wonderful sense of neighborliness among members who participate. Everyone is working together for a common cause, and everyone is reaping the benefit of this labor come harvest time.

There is just nothing quite like the feeling of watching crops develop and grow that helps folks bond together. As the plants grow, so do the connections among community members. And if your community does not already have a community garden set up, don't worry. It wouldn't be that hard for you to create one.

Keep your eyes peeled for local gardeners, and strike up a conversation with them. Give voice to your desire to establish an organic community garden, and perhaps they will become just as excited about it as you are. It takes a little courage at first to put yourself out on a limb and strike up a conversation. But I guarantee you that it will be worth it in the end.

* * *

Visit a Seed Library and Do a Crop Swap

Local seed libraries are not only a great resource—but also an opportunity to meet great people. These libraries allow visitors to "check out" seeds, as long as they promise to refill the seed packets with new seeds from their newly grown plants at the end of the growing season. It's an innovative practice, and it's just now starting to catch on in some communities.

And if you don't have a seed library in your neck of the woods, you could just as easily start your own. And while you're swapping seeds, you could do something really fun called a "crop swap," in which you and your neighbors actively trade produce amongst each other. Such a thing allows us to get back to humanity's roots—back to the days when we used to barter and trade for the things that we wanted.

Does your neighbor have their eyes on your tomatoes? Are you impressed with their rapidly growing jalapeno peppers? Well, my friends—then it's time to do a crop swap! It doesn't have to be anything official, just gather up your seeds, gather up your crops and begin exchanging with your neighbors. It's as simple as that.

* * *

Sometimes It Takes an "Ecovillage"

Have you ever heard the phrase, "Sometimes it takes a village?" The phrase is in reference to the idea that a whole community is needed to raise up our young people, rather than just an immediate family. And the same holds true for permaculture gardening as well.

Because sometimes, we need to step back and realize that we are not just part of one isolated eco-friendly garden we just planted somewhere in our backyard—but that we are actually just one small piece of an entire "ecovillage." As we get to know others who share our interest in gardening and the environment, we realize that we are not as isolated as we might have thought.

We come to understand that we have just entered into an exciting new world that is full of benefits. When members of the community actively work together to create a wholly sustainable community, an ecovillage is born. An ecovillage can range from a dozen or so people to well over one hundred.

* * *

Utilize Community Oriented Social Media Networks

Living in the digital age, we would be remiss, not to mention social media networks. Some of us might live more off the grid than others, but all it takes is the use of a common smart-phone, and one can go online and hook up with a wide variety of permaculture-oriented networks through social media.

If you need to find like-minded people, you might want to check out "Meetup.com." As described earlier, this site is actually dedicated to finding events. In the meantime, standard social media platforms such as Facebook and Twitter can be similarly utilized to find like-minded people near you.

But whatever the case may be. Whether you hook up with fellow gardeners online or you happen to bump into them in person—always try to stay as involved in your community as you can. Because as rewarding as gardening may be—everything is always better with people. Don't hesitate to be involved with your local permaculture community.

Conclusion

Here's to An Abundant Harvest!

Permanent. Sustainable. And life-enriching. Those are a few of the things that should come to mind when considering permaculture. For permaculture is not just a method of gardening but rather—a way of life. It might take a considerable change in attitude and mindset to suddenly do away with the artificial contrivances of the past and look toward nature instead for our gardening needs. Still, it's worth it in the end.

Rather than using store-bought chemicals, we can use manure. Instead of expensive garden supply brand mulch, we create our own. We might have to get down in the dirt a bit to do so. After all, it takes a bit of doing to get our worm casting compost bins up and running, but once you make a few adjustments, your permaculture garden can basically run by itself.

As you become a more thoughtful gardener, you learn how to fine-tune the whole operation to perfection. You learn environmental conditions, soil types, the benefits of plants and surrounding organisms, and you arrange all of these pieces to be in harmony with each other. Once this equilibrium is reached, the microclimates you have created will be largely autonomous.

The food forest is the perfect example of this plan in action. Because from top to bottom, food forests make use of multiple layers of resources. If set in place well, such ecological systems basically run themselves. In the end, after all, this kind of gardening is simply mimicking nature. And nature doesn't need us to tell it what to do—it's done just fine on its own!

As it pertains to permaculture, we are not trying to bang our heads against the wall, reinventing the wheel. We are simply trying to recreate the environmental systems already in place that have worked so well from the very beginning of our planet's history. As they say—if it's not broken—then don't fix it!

Just go with the natural flow of the templates that nature has already provided us with. Florida has a very unique environment, but it takes some time to understand exactly how the ecosystems of Florida work. But if you follow the precepts presented in this book, you shouldn't have any problem doing just that.

Now, put your hands in the soil and get ready for an abundant harvest!

RESOURCES

Thompson, Shein and Julie Thompson. 2013. *The Vegetable Gardener's Guide to Perma-Culture: Creating an Edible Ecosystem*

Bloom, Jessi and Dave Boehnlein.2015. *Practical Permaculture: For Home Landscapes, Your Community and the Whole Earth*

Faires, Nicole.2022. *Permaculture for Beginners: The Ultimate Guide to Natural Farming and Sustainable Living*

16 Plants That Repel Unwanted Insects (Including Mosquitoes). (2021, May 5). Treehugger. https://www.treehugger.com/plants-that-repel-unwanted-insects-4864336

A. (2016a, November 18). *Stacking Functions in Permaculture*. A Floresta Nova - A Tropical Food Forest - Brazil - Bahia - Permaculture Training.

https://aflorestanova.wordpress.com/2016/04/08/stacking-functions-in-permaculture/

A. (2018a, September 27). *Green manuring in Permaculture and Synergistic Agriculture*. Autosufficienza. https://

autosufficienza.it/en/green-manuring-in-permaculture-and-synergistic-agriculture/

A. (2022a, January 10). *What is a Permaculture Swale: Irrigate the Easy Way [+ Free Download]*. Tenth Acre Farm. https://www.tenthacrefarm.com/permaculture-swale/

A. (2022b, February 28). *5 Steps to Planting Fruit Trees.* Tenth Acre Farm. https://www.tenthacrefarm.com/5-steps-to-planting-fruit-trees/

Angelo, V. A. P. B. (2022a, January 27). *No Dig Gardening, Sustainable Gardening With Less Effort.* Deep Green Permaculture. https://deepgreenpermaculture.com/2013/10/01/no-dig-gardening/

Angelo, V. A. P. B. (2022b, February 9). *Crop Rotation Systems for Annual Vegetables.* Deep Green Permaculture. https://deepgreenpermaculture.com/2016/05/20/crop-rotation-systems-for-annual-vegetables-2/

Angelo, V. A. P. B. (2022c, April 9). *The Complete Guide to Worm Farming, Vermicomposting Made Easy.* Deep Green Permaculture. https://deepgreenpermaculture.com/2014/09/23/worm-farming/

The Basics of Companion Planting Garden Crops. (2021, November 29). The Spruce. https://www.thespruce.com/companion-planting-with-chart-5025124

Bear, J. W. (2021, October 29). *Stacking Functions for a Healthy, Vibrant Garden.* Ixchel Lunar. https://ixchel.love/stacking-functions-healthy-garden/

Bohler, D. (2017, September 5). *Permaculture Design in 5 Steps.* The Permaculture Research Institute. https://www.permaculturenews.org/2017/09/05/permaculture-design-5-steps/

Bordessa, K. (2022, March 6). *Chop and Drop Mulch: 12 Plants to Grow for Green Mulch*. Attainable Sustainable®. https://www.attainable-sustainable.net/make-mulch/

Charbonneau, J. (2018, January 17). *intercropping*. Southern Exposure Seed Exchange. https://blog.southernexposure.com/tag/intercropping/

Cook, R. (2016, January 6). *Plant – Based Insect Repellents*. The Permaculture Research Institute. https://www.permaculturenews.org/2016/01/07/plant-based-insect-repellents/

D. (2021a, March 3). *Chop-and-Drop: A Quick and Easy Way to Abundance*. Growing with Nature. https://www.growingwithnature.org/chop-and-drop/

D. (2021b, April 10). *What is No-Till Gardening or Farming (aka No-Dig): Benefits Explained*. Homestead and Chill. https://homesteadandchill.com/no-till-gardening-benefits

D. (2022c, March 14). *cowpeas*. Sticking Up for Life. https://www.stickingupforlife.com/cowpeas/

D. (2022d, March 20). *spurred butterfly pea*. Sticking Up for Life. https://www.stickingupforlife.com/spurred-butterfly-pea/

E. (2022e, March 30). *Difference Between Permaculture And Organic Gardening - Gardening Tips And Tricks*. Gardening Tips and Tricks. https://gardeningelsa.com/difference-between-permaculture-and-organic-gardening/

Eliades, A. (2016, June 3). *Perennial Plants and Permaculture*. The Permaculture Research Institute. https://www.permaculturenews.org/2012/06/06/perennial-plants-and-permaculture/

Engels, J. (2016a, January 22). *Mulching with Purpose and Precision*. The Permaculture Research Institute. https://www.permaculturenews.org/2016/01/22/mulching-with-purpose-and-precision/

Engels, J. (2016b, November 17). *How and Why to Rotate Your Annual Crops*. The Permaculture Research Institute. https://www.permaculturenews.org/2016/11/18/rotate-annual-crops/

Engels, J. (2016c, December 17). *The Magic and Mystery of Constructing a Herb Spiral and Why Every Suburban Lawn Should Have One*. The Permaculture Research Institute. https://www.permaculturenews.org/2015/04/17/the-magic-and-mystery-of-constructing-an-herb-spiral-and-why-every-suburban-lawn-should-have-one/

Engels, J. (2017, October 20). *Manure: An Overview of This Shi. . .ning Addition to the Garden*. The Permaculture Research Institute. https://www.permaculturenews.org/2017/10/20/manure-overview-shining-addition-garden/

Engels, J. (2018, February 12). *6 Beneficial Mulch Plants to Include in Your Garden*. One Green Planet. https://www.onegreenplanet.org/lifestyle/mulch-plants-include-garden/

Engels, J. (2019, October 9). *5 Reasons Why You Should Plant Cover Crops*. The Permaculture Research Institute. https://www.permaculturenews.org/2019/10/09/5-reasons-why-you-should-plant-cover-crops/

Engels, J. (2020, August 31). *Why Permaculture?* The Permaculture Research Institute. https://www.permaculturenews.org/2020/09/03/why-permaculture/

Flores, H. J. (2022, January 3). *Shrubs • Free Permaculture.* #freepermaculture. https://www.freepermaculture.com/ shrubs-hedges-and-hedgerows/

Florida Seed & Garden. (2021, September 16). *Florida's Three Growing Seasons.* https://flseeds.com/index.php/florida-growing-seasons/

Gallant, S. (2021, May 9). *The Art of Stacking Functions.* Rancho Mastatal. https://ranchomastatal.com/ blognewsletter/2016/8/15/the-art-of-stacking-functions

Gardening for Bees - Gardening Solutions - University of Florida, Institute of Food and Agricultural Sciences. (2021, October 25). Gardening for Bees. https://gardeningsolutions.ifas.ufl. edu/design/gardening-with-wildlife/gardening-for-bees.html

Gibson, A. (2018, April 19). *15 Benefits of a Herb Spiral in Your Garden.* The Micro Gardener. https://themicrogardener. com/15-benefits-of-a-herb-spiral-in-your-garden/

Gustus, D. (2022a, February 18). *Best Vermicomposting Worms for Florida.* Dengarden. https://dengarden.com/ gardening/Best-Vermicomposting-Worms-for-Florida

Gustus, D. (2022b, February 18). *Best Vermicomposting Worms for Florida.* Dengarden. https://dengarden.com/ gardening/Best-Vermicomposting-Worms-for-Florida

Gustus, D. (2022c, February 18). *Best Vermicomposting Worms for Florida.* Dengarden. https://dengarden.com/ gardening/Best-Vermicomposting-Worms-for-Florida

Hoffman, F. (2019, May 11). *Plants That Attract Beneficial Insects.* The Permaculture Research Institute. https://www. permaculturenews.org/2014/10/04/plants-attract-beneficial-insects/

https:\/\/learn.eartheasy.com\/author\/aran\/#author. (2022, February 9). *Composting: How to Make Compost using Tumblers & Bins*. Eartheasy Guides & Articles. https://learn. eartheasy.com/guides/composting/

Instructables. (2017, October 4). *How to Build a Raised Permaculture Bed*. https://www.instructables.com/How-to-Build-a-Raised-Permaculture-Bed/

J. (2018b, December 6). *The 5 Best Berries To Grow In Florida*. FL Gardening. https://www.flgardening.com/best-berries-to-grow-in-florida/

J. (2020, May 29). *Florida Vegetable Gardening For Beginners*. FL Gardening. https://www.flgardening.com/florida-vegetable-gardening/

John, P. G. (2022, March 21). *Permaculture gardening: the principles and benefits*. Passionate Gardener John. https://www.manomano.co.uk/advice/permaculture-gardening-the-principles-and-benefits-6416

K. (2021c, July 22). *How to Start a Small Herb Spiral Garden*. Kellogg Garden Organics™. https://www.kellogggarden.com/blog/gardening/how-to-start-a-small-herb-spiral-garden/

K. (2022f, January 12). *55 Trees That Are Great For Fruit Tree Guilds*. Farming My Backyard. https://farmingmybackyard.com/55-trees-that-are-great-for-fruit-tree-guilds/

Levins, M. (2011, September 29). *What are the Benefits of Permaculture? You'll Be Amazed to Know*. Gardenerdy. https://gardenerdy.com/what-are-benefits-of-permaculture/

Lindholm, H. (2021, September 23). *Everything You Need To Know About Rainwater Harvesting*. Bushman Tanks. https://bushmantanks.com.au/blog/everything-you-need-to-know-about-rainwater-harvesting/

Long, T. (2017, April 28). *How To Chop And Drop More Effectively*. The Permaculture Research Institute. https://www.permaculturenews.org/2017/04/28/chop-drop-effectively/

Marsh, J. (2021, April 27). *How to Start a Community Garden*. The Permaculture Research Institute. https://www.permaculturenews.org/2021/05/01/how-to-start-a-community-garden/

Neglia, S. (2021, August 23). *Polyculture Farming – What Is It and Why Is It Better Than Monoculture?* Outdoor Happens Homestead. https://www.outdoorhappens.com/polyculture-farming-what-is-it-and-why-is-it-better-than-monoculture/

Neubert, L. M. (2021, March 1). *Herb Spirals*. Modern Farmer. https://modernfarmer.com/2020/11/herb-spirals/

P. (2016b, April 17). *KEYHOLE GARDENS*. Permaculture Food Forest. https://permaculturefoodforest.wordpress.com/2016/04/14/keyhole-gardens/

Pennington Fertilizer. (2020, May 11). *All You Need to Know About Earthworm Castings*. Pennington.Com. https://www.pennington.com/all-products/fertilizer/resources/earthworm-castings-all-the-goodness-without-the-goo

Perfect Plants for Pollinators - Gardening Solutions - University of Florida, Institute of Food and Agricultural Sciences. (2021, September 1). Perfect Plants for Pollinators. https://gardeningsolutions.ifas.ufl.edu/design/gardening-with-wildlife/bee-plants.html

R. (2021d, April 18). *Top 10 Benefits of Worm Castings*. Iowa Worm Composting. https://www.iowawormcomposting.com/benefits-of-worm-castings/#Using_Worm_Castings

Raised Beds: Benefits and Maintenance - Gardening Solutions - University of Florida, Institute of Food and Agricultural Sciences. (2020, May 7). Raised Beds: Benefits and Maintenance. https://gardeningsolutions.ifas.ufl.edu/design/types-of-gardens/raised-beds.html

Roberts, T. (2017a, October 21). *The Importance of Guilds and Nitrogen Fixers.* The Permaculture Research Institute. https://www.permaculturenews.org/2017/10/22/importance-guilds-nitrogen-fixers/

Roberts, T. (2017b, October 21). *The Importance of Guilds and Nitrogen Fixers.* The Permaculture Research Institute. https://www.permaculturenews.org/2017/10/22/importance-guilds-nitrogen-fixers/

Rogers, N. (2021, August 25). *How To Compost In Florida [A Complete Guide].* Garden Tabs. https://gardentabs.com/how-to-compost-in-Florida/

Schauder, N. (2021, May 6). *Growing Vertically to Boost Your Harvest.* Permaculture Gardens. https://growmyownfood.com/growing-vertically/

Smith, C. (2018, February 9). *Incorporating Perennials Into Your Annual Garden (Or Working Towards Utopia).* Sow True Seed. https://sowtrueseed.com/blogs/gardening/incorporating-perennials-into-your-annual-garden-or-working-towards-utopia

StackPath. (2021, January 6). Gardening Know How. https://www.gardeningknowhow.com/composting/manures/the-benefits-of-manure-in-your-garden.htm

Thompson-Adolf, J. (2015, September 29). *The Benefits of Building a Raised Bed Garden.* The Permaculture Research

Institute. https://www.permaculturenews.org/2015/09/29/the-benefits-of-building-a-raised-bed-garden/

Waddington, E. (2020, May 29). *40 Nitrogen Fixing Plants To Grow In Your Garden*. Rural Sprout. https://www.ruralsprout.com/nitrogen-fixing-plants/

What Is Hugelkultur? Building the Ultimate Raised Bed. (2021, December 21). Almanac.Com. https://www.almanac.com/what-hugelkultur-ultimate-raised-bed

Year-round Edibles: Grow Your Food Forest. (2016, August 23). Edible South Florida. https://ediblesouthflorida.ediblecommunities.com/things-do/year-round-edibles-grow-your-food-forest

Mock, N. (2021, April 26). *How to Grow Hot Peppers*. Taste of Home. https://www.tasteofhome.com/article/how-to-grow-hot-peppers/

Made in United States
Orlando, FL
08 December 2024

55212682R00085